Praise for *Gay with God*

"Friend networks are a wonderful thing. A writer colleague reached out and invited me to meet another writer, Midge Noble. Midge then asked me to be a guest on her podcast, *GAY with GOD!*, and a beautiful friendship was born. In *Gay with God: Reclaiming My Faith, Honoring My Story,* Midge continues her incredibly meaningful work with, and for, those who have been "othered" by the church. With her presence and writing, Midge brings to life the true meaning of the inclusiveness and grace of God's love and invites others to recognize that they, too, can again step into faith and walk with others to bring much-needed growth and change into this world. Those who are LGBTQI+, those who love LGBTQI people, and those who wish to extend the love of

God to all will want to read this insightful book, and then share it everywhere!"

—**Reverend Sharon Langfeldt**
United Methodist Elder and current pastor in the United Church of Christ

"Midge and I know each other through working with the same publisher. In her delightful memoir *Gay with God* she weaves her beautiful, folksy stories to reveal a spiritual journey of hope and faith. Inspirational and insightful, her book will enlighten those who are curious as well as support and encourage those who are experiencing similar struggles with identity and acceptance."

—**Chris Davis**
Author of *Worthy: The Memoir of an Ex-Mormon Lesbian*

"'When we have the courage to walk into our story and own it,' writes Brené Brown, 'we get to write the ending.' Midge demonstrates this beautifully in her memoir *Gay with God: Reclaiming My Faith, Honoring My Story*. Through candid, relatable stories that are at once both humorous and tragic, Midge takes readers on a journey of resilience and hard-fought redemption, confronting even her most gritty and tender memories with understanding and compassion. She offers a model of what it looks like to reclaim a sense of agency, authenticity, and accountability, while still staying rooted in postures of empathy and humility. Through her 'Moments of Grace,' Midge challenges readers to wrestle with the complexities of human relationships and the paradoxes of faith. Anyone who has struggled to integrate their true self will be inspired by Midge's brave journey into self-awareness and healing."

—**Kristen Leigh Mitchell**
Master of Divinity; Spiritual Director

"I was fortunate enough to join Midge on her *GAY with GOD!* podcast. What a beautiful conversation we had about faith, sexuality, and healing from the pains of a world that doesn't understand the LGBTQ+ community. *Gay with God* and its honesty will resonate with so many. Midge's experiences, though very much her own, also belong to so many of us. And it's this commonality that will bring healing and open hearts and minds to have some restorative conversations. Midge understands the value of stories and the value of each human being as a gift from God. I can't wait for this book to get into the hands of so many who need it."

—**Katrina Kalb**
Co-Creator of Free Mom Hugs, Inc.;
Program Director/Social Media Manager;
Conversion Therapy Survivor

"If you haven't met Midge Noble or checked out her podcast *GAY with GOD!* (the same name as the book), you are in for a treat. Midge cares for people, especially those who identify on the beautiful spectrum of LGBTQ+, their families and loved ones, and even those who misunderstand or hate them. She listens deeply and compassionately. She shares openly and honestly about her faith journey and the understanding and acceptance of her own life. She knows the painful tension of faith traditions that are quick to judge and condemn and the deeper intuition that leads to an understanding that God's love is capable of embracing all people, including her.

In her book, Midge does not shy away from the doubts, fears, or painful experiences that are a part of her journey. She honors them. She applies the same compassion that she has for others to herself, which can be difficult to do. And by doing this, she lends courage to others to look at their own lives and faith journeys, or stories of coming out and coming to a loving acceptance of oneself and of others. She also speaks to the joy of living fully as yourself, as God created you to be—loved for who you are."

—**The Rev. Earnest Graham**
Episcopal Priest in the Diocese of North Carolina

"I met Midge when I moved back home. I was visiting a local brewery favorite of hers, and with the "clink" of our glasses, we struck up a conversation about being gay Christians. There are so many gay people who have left the church that it is a joy to meet another gay person of faith. I am excited to express my love for the *Gay with God* memoir because it is an important book that will enable so many more people who feel ostracized from church an opportunity to reclaim their relationship with God. May you find the joy that I found of knowing Midge and being transformed by her story."

—**Nathan Crabtree (he/him)**
Development Manager, Guilford Green Foundation & LGBTQ Center

"I've often said that folks from the LGBTQIA+ community who are able to somehow hold onto their Christian faith are rockstars, badasses, and all around spiritual heavyweights. Think about it. It takes a crazy amount of fortitude, desire, and dedication to decide to pursue a faith whose majority of followers spend an unreasonable amount of time pointing judgmental fingers at you and calling you some pretty horrific things. Midge is one of the folks who brought me to the conclusion of the badassery of queer Christians. I am so excited for the way her openness and honesty about her journey back to Christianity in the midst of her life's struggles will help others become spiritual rockstars. I'm genuinely excited for every person who picks up a copy of *Gay with God*. It's an honor to call Midge a friend."

—**Rev. Dr. Mark Sandlin**
President and Co-Executive Director of Progressive Christianity.org;
Co-Founder of The Christian Left

"*Gay with God* is Midge Noble's story of self-discovery. It is not merely entertaining and inspiring but is also instructive. In her warm, funny, and unique storytelling style, she blazes a path for others to follow. Midge is proof that you can question and doubt your faith without losing either yourself or your faith and that in fact you will, eventually, find both yourself and your faith."

—**Charles Bretan**
"The Jew" from *A Jew and a Gentile Walk into a Bar … Mitzvah*, The Podcast

"Midge Noble taught me that having the courage to share your story can literally save your life and the lives of others. *Gay with God: Reclaiming My Faith, Honoring My Story* is both an act of immense courage and a life-giving gift."

—**Ginger Campbell**
MD Host of *Graying Rainbows: Coming Out LGBT+ Later in Life*,
Author of *Are You Sure? The Unconscious Origins of Certainty*

"It's been a blessing getting to know Midge through our Publish Your Purpose cohort and being a guest on her podcast of the same name as her memoir, *Gay with God*. As someone who cares passionately about the LGBTQ+ community and creating a world where all people feel seen and loved, I'm extremely excited for her vulnerable and honest storytelling to be received by families who need it the most. Midge demonstrates that there is a way to retain faith, reclaim a relationship with God, and confidently be queer within religion."

—**Fiona Dawson**
Founder of Free Lion Productions

"I met Midge Noble at the Wild Goose Festival where her session was the recording of her podcast, *GAY with GOD!*. I introduced myself as a Catholic 'DADvocate' of LGBTQ+ children. That led to the honor of guesting on one of her later episodes where I shared the common experience of many ally Christian parents being told they have to choose between loving their faith or loving their children. Midge's memoir *Gay with God* is for all who feel in any way caught between faith and

LGBTQ+ identity. I am so grateful for Midge and her commitment to the prophetic path of celebrating the reality that spiritual living and being LGBTQ+ are not incongruent. Enjoy reading about the journey that brings us her amazing, authentic mission."

—**Greg Walton**
Catholic Composer; Speaker; Singer/Songwriter; LGBTQ+ DADvocate

"Even today in 2023, coming out as queer is difficult. Doing so within the context of any religion remains more difficult still. *Gay with God* saves lives and empowers LGBTQ folx seeking a deeper connection within circles of faith. As a longtime friend of Midge, I watched her enter St. Mary's UFMCC as a scared, scarred lesbian, seeking strength to continue and the hope of salvation. Her journey to healing began that day, and she has grown stronger and stronger through the years. Today, the passion of her faith drives her to lead other hurting people of faith through the briars and barriers that hateful religions and religious individuals and institutions erect. Her poignant memoir provides evidence that being queer with God provides persons of faith a foundation for life, a lighted path to travel, and the knowledge that they can remain faithful to themselves and to their God."

—**Kathy Kirkpatrick**
Principal (Ret.); Chair of the Democratic Party of Guilford County

Gay with God

Gay with God

Reclaiming *My* Faith, Honoring *My* Story

Midge Noble

Copyright © 2023 Midge Noble. All rights reserved.

No part of this publication shall be reproduced, transmitted, or sold in whole or in part in any form without prior written consent of the author, except as provided by the United States of America copyright law. Any unauthorized usage of the text without express written permission of the publisher is a violation of the author's copyright and is illegal and punishable by law. All trademarks and registered trademarks appearing in this guide are the property of their respective owners.

For permission requests, write to the publisher, addressed "Attention: Permissions Coordinator," at the address below.

Publish Your Purpose
141 Weston Street, #155
Hartford, CT, 06141

The opinions expressed by the Author are not necessarily those held by Publish Your Purpose.

Ordering Information: Quantity sales and special discounts are available on quantity purchases by corporations, associations, and others. For details, contact the publisher at hello@publishyourpurpose.com.

Edited by: Malka Wickramatilake & Nancy Graham-Tillman
Cover design by: Designerbility
Typeset by: Medlar Publishing Solutions Pvt Ltd., India

ISBN: 979-8-88797-035-6 (hardcover)
ISBN: 979-8-88797-034-9 (paperback)
ISBN: 979-8-88797-036-3 (ebook)

Library of Congress Control Number: 2023903629

First edition, October 2023.

The information contained within this book is strictly for informational purposes. The material may include information, products, or services by third parties. As such, the Author and Publisher do not assume responsibility or liability for any third-party material or opinions. The publisher is not responsible for websites (or their content) that are not owned by the publisher. Readers are advised to do their own due diligence when it comes to making decisions.

Publish Your Purpose is a hybrid publisher of non-fiction books. Our mission is to elevate the voices often excluded from traditional publishing. We intentionally seek out authors and storytellers with diverse backgrounds, life experiences, and unique perspectives to publish books that will make an impact in the world. Do you have a book idea you would like us to consider publishing? Please visit PublishYourPurpose.com for more information.

Dedication

*I dedicate this memoir to the person who saw my pain,
my fake bravado, my insecurities, my ugly parts,
and the good parts that I could not see myself.*

She stood by me through my confusion, conflicts, and fears.

She loved and supported me through it all.

I love you, my beloved, my soul mate, my best friend—my wife.

Back-to-back and front-to-front …

Always, Turtle Dove

Two Turtle Doves

Contents

Foreword xxi
Letter to You, Dear Reader xxv

Part 1: My Family

1	Meet My Momma! 3
2	Meet My Daddy! 7
3	Here I Am, World! 13
4	Am I Worthy? 19
5	The Girls 25
6	The Golden Boy, or Not! 29
7	North Marries South! 35

Part 2: Trials

8   Jesus Facade 51
9   Testing the Call 55
10 The Slough of Despond 61
11 The Land of Contrast, Dysentery, and Homesickness 71
12 The Eggs Fell Out of the Basket. 79
13 Berkshire Christian College 85
14 Major Crush 95

Part 3: Searching

15 Wild-Haired Boy 105
16 The Love Story Begins. 109
17 Crisis Creates Change 121
18 Broken Trust. 125
19 GRE 133
20 Life Emerging 139
21 Dani 145

Part 4: Rebirth

22 Life after Graduate School 155
23 Out of the Darkness .161
24 I Died at Age Thirty .169
25 Reclaiming My Faith .175

CONTENTS

Epilogue 183
Afterword. 187
Closing Letter 191
Acknowledgments 193
About the Author 197
Connect with Midge. 199
Listen to The Podcast. .201
Hire Midge 203
Gay With God *Book Club Questions* 205
Bibliography 207

Foreword

There's a face to every issue. When the faces and voices of those who are impacted by decisions made in pastors' offices are obscured, or when hollow rhetoric isn't challenged, we intentionally create division and inequity and therefore compromise their safety. Those of us on the receiving end of these decisions, choices, and laws can feel powerless. While that's the goal, it's not the truth.

We each have personal power in telling our truths. It's through the telling of our stories, putting a face and voice to these issues, that we shift culture and help heal that sense of separation. That's what Midge Noble is doing in her book *Gay with God*. In it, she exudes authenticity in telling her truth and puts her vulnerability out there to be the spiritual mentor she needed as she rode the roller coaster of her journey.

With her podcast of the same name, she's been reaching the lonely hearts who may not have anyone around them to support them, talk to them, ask questions, figure things out, and help them develop their own sense of self and identity. Midge is that link, that lifesaver that so many youth and adults alike need to survive.

In 2023, The Trevor Project revealed that there are over 500 bills actively targeting the LGBTQIA+ community. We have to understand that the people in power who are driving this intentional harm and the erasure of the basic human right to exist are dependent on firing up Christians to support their dangerous plans. Christians are pressured to obey and are being used as pawns, while families with LGBTQIA+ and questioning friends and family members are needing their love, support, and protection.

Midge provides much-needed guidance and invites readers to their own "come to Jesus moment" through her story. I know the power of sharing one's story. As a guest on the *GAY with GOD!* podcast, I shared my difficult coming out story, noting that I considered suicide. Raised in a conservative Christian denomination, I believed the lies that God wouldn't love me if I felt love for another woman. Thankfully, in the midst of the depression and ideation, I remembered a silly poster from when I was in second grade that read, "God don't make no junk." Grammatically incorrect, but spiritually profound.

I live my life authentically. I live my truth. It really does get better, and readers will see that come through in Midge's story too. Readers may feel conflict and tension. We've been pulled in many directions as our churches have become more insistent on framing God's natural design of a wide variety of human experiences as something to be squashed rather than something that God is putting in our hearts. Just know that this is part of the process, and go through the work.

We must not project our fears or ignorance onto LGBTQIA+ people. We must not cross the line and punish someone for living their truth. We must not project our confusion on LGBTQIA+ folx because we simply don't understand their experience. Understanding is not required in order to love and support someone. When we make space

FOREWORD

for people to find themselves and their own relationship with the universe, they will be free. And so will we. Free to be.

Thank you, Midge, for this labor of love and for being a living example of why it's all worth it.

—**Kim Clark (she/her)**
Diversity, Equity, and Inclusion Communications Speaker
and Consultant at Kim Clark Communications, Inc.
Co-Author of *The Conscious Communicator: The Fine Art of Not Saying Stupid Sh*t*
Producer of *God and Gays: Bridging the Gap*

Letter to you, Dear Reader

Dear Reader,

So, you have picked up my memoir! Thank you! Full disclosure: the title of this book wasn't always going to be what it is today. Originally, I was going to call it *Gay with God: Returning To The Pew without Puking!* because that is 100 percent how I felt as I journeyed back to my relationship with God. While many people laughed at it and loved that subtitle, many others thought that it might keep some people from reading the book. So I changed it to reflect my whole journey. Even though I was raised in an Advent Christian church and had a grandfather and uncle who were ministers, I wound up leaving the church because I was told that homosexuals were abominations and that I would go to hell. I still tried to keep my spiritual connection to God. The word "God," however, became increasingly difficult to say or connect with, so I became spiritual and not religious and started using the name "Creator of All that Is" as my connection to the Divine. It took me many years to reclaim the name of God and my faith. My journey back has been difficult, confusing, painful, and rewarding.

I want this book to resonate with the people who question whether they can be gay *and* have a relationship with the God of their understanding. If my story can be a light to them, I have fulfilled my calling.

This book is for you if you

- identify as LGBTQIA+,
- have been wounded by the church,
- have struggled to retain or reclaim your faith,
- are ready to come out and want to see how one person made it through,
- love someone who is gay and fear for their salvation, and/or
- are an open-minded human and show compassion for others by wanting to learn more about people who may not be like you.

You can count on this book to be an honest, raw, flawed, and—to the best of my ability—accurate account of my journey. I have discovered that some of my memories are crystal clear, as if these events happened just yesterday. Other memories, including my age and the linear timetable, are a bit cloudier.

As you read my struggles, my dark nights of the soul, my joys, my accomplishments, and my lessons, I want you to know that things can get better for you. I wrote this memoir to show you an example of how life got better for me. It is my honor if my book keeps you going when you feel like giving up.

At the writing of this letter, I am a 63-year-old, white, cisgender female who identifies as gay or lesbian. I love my wife of over 30 years, our cabin, and our fur babies, as well as hiking, cooking, serving my parish, podcasting, and coaching.

Throughout the book, you will be introduced to my family at different intervals of our lives. My family does not always look good and,

LETTER TO YOU, DEAR READER

for that matter, neither do I. That is because none of us were trained in being us before we were thrown together into our Noble family. We all made mistakes. We all had very definite opinions about what was right and wrong and, as you can imagine, we clashed at times. We still do!

A quote from Anne Lamott that I read in Jenn T. Grace's book *House on Fire* kept me focused when I felt like sugarcoating the past: *"You own everything that happened to you. Tell your stories. If people wanted you to write warmly about them, they should have behaved better."*

FYI, with the exception of Father Joe and Mom Flynn, I did change the names of family, friends, and acquaintances because, even though these are *my* memories, it is up to each person to tell their own story. If you want to read all of the juicy stories of my life that are not included in this memoir, watch my website for all the untold stories at https://gaywithgod.com.

A few more things I want you to know:

- You are beloved!
- You don't have to earn it. You don't have to be a certain religion. You don't have to be perfect.
- You are still beloved and worthy of all good things.

Namaste,

Midge

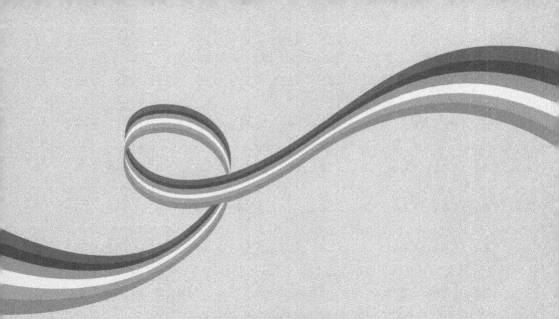

All shall be well, and
all shall be well, and
all manner of things
shall be well.

—JULIAN OF NORWICH

My Family

Part 1

Meet My Momma!

Momma, along with her two younger brothers, was raised in Illinois by my maternal grandparents, whom I called Grandma and Grandpa.

Momma had a great figure with a thin waist, which she highlighted by wearing wide belts and poodle skirts. After she had her third child, she began to struggle with her weight. She put herself through years of home exercising, buying every piece of equipment we could afford and snacking on Ayds diet chews like they were candy. Being that I was the chubby child, Momma modeled for me how to work out and watch what I ate, and she expected me to follow her regimen.

Having grown up in very close proximity to her aunts, uncles, and cousins, Momma had the opportunity to share holidays, birthdays, and special events with the entire family. She remembers that time of her life as full of laughter, joy, and love among everyone. She learned to play chords on the piano, she sang in the choir with her mom, and she loves the 1950s, including musicals, dancing, and Shirley Temple and Doris Day movies. She has stood by her belief that the 1950s were the best of times, remembering going to clubs and dancing and people leaving their homes unlocked. She believes that all the drugs, crime, and murders we have today were just not part of that era.

Momma would sometimes talk about herself and say, "I never should have been a mother," and that she was really "angry" when she learned she was pregnant with me. She would go on to say, "I was angry the entire time I was pregnant with you. Of course I love you now, but I really didn't want to be pregnant with you." *I wonder if I, as a fetus, could feel all that anger from my mom during her pregnancy.*

I remember one night, though, when I was little, Momma came into my bedroom to rub my back when I was having trouble falling asleep. That memory serves as a reminder to me that she had some capacity to nurture me.

There was one secret (probably more) in Momma's family that neither she nor her siblings were aware of when they were younger: their dad had been living with bipolar disorder. Momma believes that Grandma must have lived a very painful life protecting Grandpa's dignity, and she remembers that Grandma would just laugh and make jokes when it came to Grandpa's erratic behaviors. I particularly remember one time when I asked her about this.

"You know, we never knew, we just never knew," Momma answered.

"Yeah, I hear that," I said. "Grandma did a really good job of protecting everybody from that, but I wonder how it really did affect the family."

"I think it really affected Grandma. She was the one who kept that secret, and she was the one who had to deal with him behind closed doors. I can remember only one time, one time that … um … that I felt that something was really wrong." She continued,

I had chicken pox when I was younger, and I scratched it like I wasn't supposed to, and on one side of my nose I got a little, teeny, tiny scar, and I could never remember what side of my nose it was on. Well somehow, at the kitchen table, that conversation came up, and my dad reached over across the table and took his fingernail and swiped me on the side of my nose where that scar was. And it hurt and I started cryin' and I got up and left the table, and … uh … he followed me. And then he said, "I'm sorry, I'm sorry. I just didn't want you to ever forget what side that scar was on anymore. I was just trying to be helpful." Well, I probably will never forget now what side of the nose my scar is on.

Following the story, Momma said, "But that was that."
"Well, wait a minute, what did Grandma do?" I asked.
Momma sat there for a minute and said, "I don't think she did anything. I think she might have said, 'Oh Walter,' but I don't think she said anything."
"Why do you think she didn't say anything?"
"She probably didn't want to get in the middle of it."
Momma and I sat in silence for a while. I was thinking, and perhaps she was too, about how much pain Grandma must have been in, suffering, staying quiet, and never getting support from her family. I also thought how sad for my mom that, instead of supporting her, Grandma chose to not respond to prevent a bad situation from escalating.

When Grandma later had a stroke, it made Grandpa's mental health issues dangerous to her daily survival. Momma specifically asked me to pray for Grandma to regain her ability to speak so that she could get out of the nursing home. Whenever something went wrong in her life, Momma always blamed God for not answering prayers, and she would sometimes ask me to explain to her why God did things. At the age of 10, I didn't have the deep theological insight to satisfy her, yet I was tasked with asking for a cure for Grandma. I can never be sure whether the prayers were answered or Grandma chose not to speak so she could stay safe from her husband.

As I look back now, Momma's family was not all laughter and love. Her family had secrets, undiagnosed mental illness, shame, and incredibly scary times for my grandma; Momma just didn't know it then. Though Momma could tell Grandma anything, the only way for Grandma to protect Momma was by not disclosing things or confiding in her.

At the writing of this memoir, Momma is 87 years old, a breast cancer survivor, and living with my sister and her family.

A Moment of Grace

Momma loved me as best as she could. She thinks I am wise and funny, and she enjoys my company. She has always wanted what is best for me and for me to be happy, even when she didn't have the power to do it herself.

Meet My Daddy!

My dad was born in Cooper's Creek, West Virginia, to my paternal grandparents, who I call Maw Maw and Paw Paw. Daddy had two younger brothers. He grew up on a dairy farm and was always expected to get his chores done before supper. It was Paw Paw's rule that if you were not at the table when a meal was served, you didn't eat.

Daddy was an excellent athlete and played a variety of sports. He was often late to supper because of away games or after-school practices. Maw Maw would hide a tin pan of leftovers from supper in the back of the oven so that Daddy would have something to eat when he got home.

Growing up during the draft, Daddy decided to enlist in the Navy so he wouldn't be drafted into a branch he didn't want to be in. He was stationed on the carrier USS Leyte during the Korean War. He did get to play basketball for the Navy team and once scored 50 points himself in one game! Though he could have gone pro, he wanted an education first, and the US Navy would pay for his college.

While Daddy was in the Navy, Paw Paw felt the call to be a preacher. While Daddy was deployed, the Noble family moved from the farm in West Virginia to Maryland. Since the place of his birth was no longer where the family lived, Daddy felt he never really got to return "home" after he completed his four years in the Navy.

Once Daddy returned home, Paw Paw wanted him to go into ministry and encouraged him to attend Aurora College, one of the Advent Christian colleges at that time. Daddy didn't feel called to preach, however, and graduated with a teaching certificate instead.

While he was at Aurora College, Daddy continued to play basketball and baseball. He once received the team ball in a game after pitching a no-hitter. Unfortunately, in another game, a line drive came back at Daddy before he could blink. The baseball caught him right in the eye socket and his eyeball popped out! Years later, when I asked him what he did about this, Daddy nonchalantly said, "I popped it back in!"

Going on to teach and coach at South Caldwell High School, Daddy was loved by his students and ball players. He was a tough coach and expected a lot out of his players, but it paid off when they won an SD7 conference championship! Emulating Dean Smith's coaching style, Daddy would say that if you cut him, he would bleed Carolina blue. That was the one and only thing he and I always agreed on—the Tar Heels! If Daddy and I didn't share our love of the Tar Heels, I don't know what we would have had in common.

One thing that worried me, though, was that he would often miss church to watch a Carolina game. So I always advocated that we pray before meals and do family devotions. When Daddy turned those requests down, I felt that I had failed God.

Daddy also adopted Coach Dean Smith's philosophy that basketball is a team sport. He didn't like showboats and told his players that they either play as a team or they don't play at all. One night, he benched his star point guard because he wouldn't run the plays. When we left the gym that rainy night, a man was waiting for Daddy. Daddy instructed Momma to take us to the car and, craning to see through a foggy window, I witnessed a man hold a knife to Daddy and start yelling at him for benching his son. I don't know what Daddy said to the man, but he was able to get back in the car and we took off.

Momma asked, "What did he say?"

"Not in front of the kids. Let's just get out of here," Daddy replied.

Daddy could be very moody, depressed, and angry. He was known to stomp and throw clipboards and chairs in the gym when, in his opinion, the refs didn't make the right call. When we would drive up to the high school to watch him coach a game, there had to be complete silence so he could go over his game plan in his head, over and over and over. If the team lost a game, there would be complete silence all the way home because he was devastated, revisiting in his mind every play and choice he had made.

Anytime my dad was challenged, including when we would disagree, he would go to a very dark place. When I was about 10 years old, for instance, I asked to do something and, like any other kid, kept badgering him when he refused me. Daddy turned to me and said, "If you're not going to listen, you don't need a daddy. You would just be better off without me here." With that comment, he left the house and took off in the car. I was scared that he might not come back because, in those days, his erratic behavior had given us pause to think that he might even kill himself.

It was an excruciating amount of time before he returned. When he did come back, he sat in his chair, turned on the TV, and said nothing. He never explained where he went, and there was never an apology. During that whole time of him leaving and coming back to only sit in silence, Momma didn't say much except, "You should have listened."

I felt responsible. I played that over and over in my head. What if he had killed himself? I would be to blame.

What I didn't understand at the time was that my dad had a drinking problem. He had started drinking in the Navy and then continued through college, his drinking getting heavier as the years passed. He had promised Momma that there would never be liquor in the house once they were married, and he kept that promise—until we kids started growing up. Beer would appear in the house when we would go away to attend a week-long Advent Christian camp every summer. It was supposed to be a "family" camp, but our parents never attended.

The truth was that Daddy never stopped drinking. He just didn't do it at home when we were there. Before a game, he would go to a coaching buddy's house where they would have a beer with dinner, and on the weekends he would drink while he played cards with friends. When Daddy drank, he drank until there was nothing left to drink.

I remember being stunned when I found out Daddy drank alcohol. It opened a whole place inside of me where trust, lies, and pain were brought to the surface. Once, when I was in high school, Daddy found out I had tried cigarettes and became so angry—even though he had been smoking for as long as I could remember. When he smelled beer on my breath for the first time, his statement was, "We raised you better than that. We don't drink, why do you think you have to?" All those expectations, all those higher-than-thou standards. I didn't care if he drank; I cared that I was held to a higher, impossible-to-attain standard—one that he had not achieved.

When I think back on how hard Daddy was on himself, I imagine how difficult it must have been for him to live a life of lies. Outwardly, he showed himself as someone who lived with high standards and morals. But he knew the truth of what he was hiding. Drinking and smoking didn't make him a bad person. He was a man with low self-confidence who didn't have the ability to be authentic. That must have taken a very great toll on his psyche.

Daddy was a stoic man. He had a lot of headaches and leg cramps but was never one to stay home from teaching because he was sick. By the end of his career, he had accumulated so much sick leave that he was able to retire a year early.

MEET MY DADDY!

On February 4th, 1998, Daddy died of a massive heart attack on an emergency room bed. He had lived with emphysema for years and had two collapsed lungs.

> ### A Moment of Grace
>
> I know that Daddy was raised in a home with strict rules and judgment. Even with his lack of self-worth, he provided us with a safe home and exceeded the parenting role models that were given to him. Toward the end of his life, he welcomed me and my family (referring to those I had chosen to love as "family") to a family reunion. Though the reunion never happened before his death, he was beginning to open.

Here I Am, World!

I have been told that I was born in Hickory, North Carolina, at the Hickory Memorial Hospital. I weighed six pounds, nine ounces and was eighteen inches long. Why is this important? For two reasons: 1) this is the lowest weight I have ever been, and weight, as it turns out, has been an ongoing theme for me, and 2) this is proof that I did go home with parents who have verification that I am part of the Noble gene pool. This is something that I would wonder about throughout my life because I have never really had the same feelings, thoughts, or reactions as anyone in my family. In my opinion, I didn't look like them, I didn't like all the things they liked, and I always felt as if I didn't belong. I knew that I was different, but I just couldn't put my finger on why.

I was born in the rural South in the late 1950s, on a Wednesday. My parents had decided to name me Michelle with two ls. Then, Momma changed her mind because she didn't like the way it looked, so I became Michele with one L. This causes some people a lot of problems. They either can't spell or can't say my name correctly. My middle name is Ann without an E. Momma nicknamed me Midge after hearing her friend call her daughter, also named Michelle, Mitch. Momma thought she had called her a "bitch" and didn't want anyone to make that mistake, so when she would talk to my sister about me, she would call me "Midgee." My blonde hair was so light that my dad would call me "Towhead." I still don't know why. I was, and still am, very fair-skinned; I flash-burn and never tan. My face turns really red when I am hot, anxious, or excited, or when I am in front of people as a speaker or lay-reader at church.

One month after I was born, I was dedicated in the church by Paw Paw, who had a huge influence on how my parents raised my siblings and me. Paw Paw was an old-school, fire-and-brimstone preacher. He didn't believe in playing cards, dating, or missing church—ever—unless you were dead or dying, and he would call on Sunday if we missed church to find out who was so sick. He also believed in praying at the table before meals, which we did whenever he visited. The confusing part was that those rules about not playing cards and praying before meals didn't apply when Paw Paw wasn't there. My dad explained that he honored his father's wishes when his father was present. It still feels hypocritical.

When I was little, my mom would tell me that "Wednesday's child is full of woe," being sure to remind me that Wednesday was the day I was born. There does seem to be a discrepancy in her assessment, though, because the poem "Significance of the Days" that is in my baby book reads this way:

> Monday's child is fair of face
> Tuesday's child is full of grace
> Wednesday's child is never sad
> Thursday's child is merry and glad
> Friday's child is loving and giving

HERE I AM, WORLD!

> Saturday's child earns a very good living
> The child that is born on the Sabbath day is
> Good and loving and wise and gay.[1]

As it turns out, I think I should have been born on the Sabbath!

I don't know why Momma would tell me these things, as I was too young to understand an adult's perspective. Since I had not learned to read yet, these words in my baby book meant nothing to me either, so Momma's truth was the gospel and I immediately internalized her version.

It wasn't until later that I came to understand that my older sister, *older* being the key word, had been born 13 months before me, yet it was Momma's pregnancy with me that had made her so angry. She was young at the time and away from the support of her family, and I understand how hard it must have been to have both a child in diapers and a newborn. Unfortunately, though, I had no knowledge as to why Momma was so angry about my birth, so in lieu I developed my own theories based on stories she told me as I was growing up. *It was evident that I wasn't wanted or cherished.*

When I was brought home from the hospital, Grandma came down from Illinois to help Momma out with my sister and four-day old me. We had a very tiny house that included a kitchen, a living room, two bedrooms, a bathroom, and a laundry room. Every room was very small with limited space. The only place to change a baby, according to my mom, was the kitchen table.

One morning, Momma laid me down on a blanket on top of the kitchen table to change me before realizing that she didn't have a diaper, so she called for Grandma to come watch me. Assuming Grandma had

---

[1] The author of this version is not listed, but the nursery rhyme is adapted from the original: Anna Eliza Bray, *Traditions, Legends, Superstitions, and Sketches of Devonshire: On the Borders of the Tamar and the Tavy, Illustrative of Its Manners, Customs, History, Antiquities, Scenery, and Natural History*, Volume II (London: John Murray, 1838), 287–288.

heard her—the house was tiny after all, so how could one not hear?—she left me on the kitchen table to search for a diaper. But Grandma had not heard her. It is fair to say that I shouldn't have been in much danger. I was only four days old, and I couldn't roll over, crawl, or walk off the table. But no one anticipated Polly, my 13-month-old sister, walking into the kitchen at that moment. The edge of the blanket I was on hung delicately off the side of the table, and it caught Polly's eye. She took it with her two small hands and pulled. Down went the blanket, and down I went with it. BOOM! I hit the floor. I am not sure who got there first, but when Momma and Grandma got to the kitchen, they found me on the floor, screaming at the top of my little lungs. Though Momma called the doctor, apparently head injuries were not really taken too seriously back then. The doctor said that if I was breathing and crying, I would be okay. *Really?!* Momma trusted the doctor, and I was never evaluated.

The next time I was left alone with Polly (yes there was a next time), Momma didn't have Grandma in the house to help. I was still quite young and had not yet started crawling. Momma went to hang out clothes on the line while we stayed inside, because apparently it was too cold for us to be outside with her and she feared us getting sick. Laying me down on the carpet in the living room, Momma carefully explained to my sister—still a mere toddler herself—how to help me if I started to cry: "If Midgee starts to cry, she's probably hungry. I want you to go to the refrigerator, open the door, get Midgee's bottle, give it to her, and then come get me."

Now, I don't know whether my sister appeared to be academically gifted during this time of her youth, but this sounds like a lot of steps to follow for someone so young.

Momma went outside and, to no surprise, I started to cry. So, Polly walked to the refrigerator, opened the door, took out the bottle, pushed it aside … and grabbed a hot dog! When Momma came back into the house, she heard me gagging—Polly was trying to shove a hot dog down my throat! As if falling off a table as an infant and nearly being choked to death by my well-meaning sister wasn't bad enough …

…Back in the day, as some of you will recall, our moms used heavy metal razors with real razor blades. Yep, you see it coming, don't you? Momma once forgot that she left her razor on the side of the tub. I was mobile by then, around three years old, and had walked into the bathroom and picked up the razor by the bladed side. My sister knew that was dangerous and wanted to protect me from hurting myself, so she grabbed the handle to take it from me. When she did that, the razor ripped through my tiny middle finger on my right hand. I have a vague memory of that incident and still bear a very bumpy scar on that finger.

In Polly's defense, she did tell me, "Well, I didn't want you to get cut."

"Thank you?"

I don't blame my sister for these events. She was too young to make the kind of decisions she was put in a position to make. I also have compassion for my mom, who was alone with an infant and a very young toddler. With Daddy teaching school all day and coaching all night, Momma must have felt like a single mom. There was no one to help her if she had to leave the house.

My adult brain knows that accidents happen but, growing up, my young heart interpreted these stories differently.

My sister and I were glued at the hip, until she started school a year before I did. My parents and my little brother always referred to us as "The Girls." I wondered sometimes whether my brother even really knew our names!

When we were little, Momma would often dress us alike because we were so close in age. We played together and did pretty much everything together. The only thing we didn't do together was get mumps. Polly got the mumps, and though we still did everything together and even shared a bed, to this day I have never had the mumps. If you just thought that I had better knock on wood so I don't get mumps now, you betcha; I just did!

Despite the chaos that seemed to often be at hand, there were also truly wonderful moments living at 23rd Avenue. Our home was laid out as a big square so that each room opened into another. It was a great place to ride our tricycles inside, and Polly and I loved doing this! We also loved using the swing set that Daddy had put up on a little knoll in the backyard. For whatever reason, he never anchored the legs of the set into the ground properly. At first, it wasn't a big deal, but as we got older, Polly and I would have swinging contests to see who could get those legs to come off the ground!

A Moment of Grace

I know now that my mom was stretched to capacity as a stay-at-home mom. One who had no support. My sister was only 13 months older than me, so there was no way she had the capability to care for me. I am grateful I survived.

Am I Worthy?

Most of my life, I have felt unseen and unworthy and questioned whether I was loved. For me, feeling worthy is connected to feeling that I belong. I wanted my family to want me, I wanted to be loved by God, and somewhere along the way I connected the two.

I was four-and-a-half-years old when Momma got pregnant with my brother. Throughout her pregnancy, I would hear comments from my dad such as, "I hope we get it right this time," "We've tried twice and got it wrong; maybe this time we'll have a boy," and "If we don't get a boy this time, I might have to kill myself." I don't know how often he said that last part, I just know that I heard it and internalized it.

The night my brother was born, Paw Paw came home from the hospital and announced, "Midgee, Polly, you have a new baby coming to your house."

I immediately asked, "Is it a boy or a girl?"

"Well Midgee, it's a boy! You girls have a baby brother."

"Thank God," I said. "Now Daddy won't have to kill himself!"

There was stunned silence after the words came out of my mouth, and I saw all the adults looking at each other. Now that my brother—the "Golden Boy," as my sister and I would refer to him for years after that—had been born, I felt so relieved! I decided to ask another question, which would define the beginning of my faith journey at the tender age of five.

"Paw Paw, who made God?"

Paw Paw had only one answer: "Go to bed."

At first I didn't understand what I had done wrong. Was I being punished? Why wasn't I supposed to ask a question? I also didn't know why Paw Paw wouldn't tell me who made God. Was it a secret? Was it bad? That one moment shut the door on my exploration. Although I had always wanted that question answered, I knew definitively that that night was not when I was going to find out who God's parents were.

Growing up around a minister gave me the opportunity to go to church often. Anytime Paw Paw ministered at a church within driving distance for us, we were expected to attend his service. I grew up with such a conflicting view of God and church, though. My grandfather preached that you would go to Hell if you didn't get saved and didn't do exactly as the Bible said. He was convinced that the Bible was the inspired word of God, and because God said it, I was to believe it, and that settled it. Again, I learned not to ask questions and to just accept the words as they are written.

In Paw Paw's later years, he was convinced that we were living in the end of times and Jesus was coming any minute. So in my youth, I feared the thought of going to Hell. And in doubting that I was good enough, I knew I probably wouldn't go to Heaven. I remembered hearing the story of Saul, who walked the dusty roads of Damascus. He went through a conversion, turning from the wicked man he was to being named Paul after finding God's favor. At the time, the only way I could relate to that story was to walk a dusty road and serve God, so

I began to invest all my energy in being the pious Christian I thought I was supposed to be.

My plan was fear-based, and I successfully kept that inner truth hidden from myself. I would refer to it as my calling. I convinced myself that I had really been called by God to the mission field, and I spent the rest of my youth preparing for that mission. First, however, I had to survive what would be a roller coaster of emotions and times when I really didn't think I would survive.

Looking back, one pivotal moment that showed me why I felt unworthy in my family happened when my brother Ethan was just a toddler and I was around five-and-a-half-years old. We were playing in the living room while Momma was washing dishes in the kitchen, which was across from us. I don't remember Ethan and I being very loud or particularly rambunctious, but all of a sudden Momma came pounding across the kitchen floor and into the living room. She had on her green sweater with the sleeves pushed up to her elbows, and soapy water was running down her arm. She pointed her finger a hair from my face, and with a red face and her death-ray glare directly on me, she screamed, "I can't wait for you to grow up and get out of this house!"

I could barely breathe and didn't want to make a sound. I was so scared of her in that moment and didn't know what to think. Her words seared through my heart as if she had stabbed me with a knife. She turned around, went back to the dishes, and never said another word about it.

I turned to Ethan, whose eyes were fixated on me, and said, "It's okay. We just need to be really, really quiet."

I felt very protective of Ethan and didn't want him to be as scared as I was. I hoped he would be too young to remember what had just happened. I wanted him to believe that Momma loved us, that she loved me, but in that moment I believed she didn't love me, and that became burned into my heart. I didn't belong; she didn't want me here; she couldn't wait for me to be gone. I wasn't worthy of her love.

The memory of that moment has resonated with me throughout my life and, even as I write about it now, I can see and feel it as clearly as if it were yesterday. I have been deeply impacted by those words and the rage on her face. I felt unloved and dispensable. Whatever I had done was bad enough that her love for me had been altered. She wanted me grown and she wanted me out of the house.

But I was too young to get out of that house. I had many more years to live there and know I wasn't wanted. I became a people pleaser and peacemaker, probably to be liked and to stay under the radar of Momma's anger with me. Her previous stories of being angry the whole time she was pregnant with me morphed into my belief that *she wasn't just angry she was pregnant with me; she must have really hated me when she was pregnant. She must really hate me now.*

I knew then that, as soon as I was able, I would get out of that house! In the meantime, I had to wall off the pain so that I didn't feel it every single minute. I coped by shutting down, not feeling, and trying to be perfect.

Kids listen and are impacted by what they hear and what they see. Trauma is not always physical. When it is emotional, the wounds are not seen by others and are not attended to. Even though the emotional wounds cannot make us bleed on the outside, the holes in our hearts always leave scars. My wounds altered many of my choices and my belief in who I was.

I guess during those years, I was given a lot of opportunities to go with the flow and learn to be more accepting of change, but I didn't do well with that. I liked things to stay the same because I knew what to do and how to act as long as things stayed constant.

A Moment of Grace

I believe my parents did the best they could. Unfortunately, it wasn't what was best for me. They sacrificed and took care of our physical needs. I understand that now, and I send them love. Paw Paw was loved by many parishioners, respected by my daddy, and feared by me. He couldn't answer my questions because there is no conclusive evidence of who made God. It must have been difficult for him to not have an answer for me. I still want to know!

The Girls

Polly was so skinny as a kid that I used to joke that if she turned sideways, she would disappear. Compared to her, I always looked fat. It didn't help that Maw Maw would buy us identical outfits at Christmas, and in the same size! She would always say the same thing: "Well Midgee, it looks like you have gained weight this year."

By the way, an entire outfit of a large flower print from head to toe on a chubby girl is never a good look. Add to that the fact that I couldn't always button or zip the pants up. If I did that, I couldn't breathe and my body would bulge at the seams. *These Christmas "reveals" had a direct and long-lasting effect on how I saw myself.*

Polly and I were each other's only playmates. We did most things together, including getting into trouble. We couldn't be quiet when it was bedtime, for one thing. We were supposed to go to bed, stop talking, and go to sleep, but that was all the directive we needed to get the giggles! Of course, we found everything funny, and it would take several warnings for us to finally settle down and sleep.

Polly was very emotionally distant. She didn't like to be hugged and even resisted me when I would try to hug her. She has always been quick to tell me what to do and not do, and I would do it or not do it, including not hugging her. I had fully assumed the role of people pleaser and peacemaker in our family, roles that would prove to have dangerous consequences for me.

One evening, when Polly was 13, I was 12, and Ethan was seven, we were eating supper at the kitchen table while Daddy was sitting on his favorite recliner in the living room with a TV tray on his lap. Momma was in the kitchen at the other side of the bar, standing up and eating while she cleaned as well. Our dog Chipper was outside tied up to a bush in the backyard, as tying him up was Daddy's solution to prevent him from getting hit by the cars speeding down the road in front of the house.

A thunderstorm was brewing.

Polly stood up at the first clap of thunder and said, "We need to go get Chipper in the basement before he gets struck by lightning."

I immediately stood up and went downstairs with her, while Momma stood in silence. I don't know what made me so gung-ho to help—the last time I had experienced such a bad storm was four years earlier when we had been at our grandparents' cabin. A lightning bolt came out of the TV and hit three of the cabin walls, sending us kids onto the floor. I remembered this and was terrified, but there I was, on the basement landing, with Polly barking orders at me: "Go untie Chipper from the bush!"

I went out into the storm while she stood at the door. Chipper had wrapped himself around the trunk of the bush and was pulling with great force as he tried to get inside, while I was fumbling to untangle the chain. I was trying to find the clip to release him when thunder boomed over my head and a lightning flash momentarily blinded me.

I can't believe I'm holding onto metal in a storm. I hate this! I'm going to die under this stupid bush! Oh my God ... help me, please help me! I was screaming to myself.

"Hurry up!" Polly yelled.

"You come do it!" I screamed back, but the sound of my voice was absorbed by another clap of thunder. I was shaking and soaked. It seemed like forever, but I finally got the chain undone and freed Chipper, who immediately ran to the door—with me right behind him.

"Grab his stuff and water!" came another command from Polly.

I turned from the door and grabbed a bone and the water bowl. Simultaneously, a flash of lightning and a deafening boom scared me so bad that I dropped everything. I screamed and ran for the door.

"Well, at least get his water," Polly yelled before I got to the door, "or he'll thirst to death!"

I grabbed the upside-down bowl, ran to the faucet, and turned it on. Immediately, lightning struck the spigot, bounced off it, and struck me, knocking me back against the brick wall of the house. I screamed a blood-curdling, Alfred-Hitchcock-like scream, and my sister slammed the basement screen door shut. I ran to the door but, with its metal handle, it took three attempts for me to even get a grip on it and finally pull the door open.

Once inside, I saw Polly standing there, holding on to Chipper. All she could say was, "Don't touch me, don't touch me," and I was screaming, "I was struck by lightning! I was struck by lightning!"

Apparently we were making too much noise, because Daddy came bounding down the stairs, grabbed me by the shoulders, and said while shaking me, "What is wrong with you?"

"I was struck by lightning! I really was!" I exclaimed.

He looked me up and down and then said, "Well, go finish supper."

I just stared at him and then quietly walked up the basement stairs. Neither Polly nor Daddy followed me. I walked through the kitchen, went into the dining room, sat in my spot, looked at my plate, and just sat there. *I think I had disassociated. I only remember staring and not being aware of thoughts or feelings.*

All of a sudden I heard, "Is there anything wrong?" Momma's voice brought me back to the present.

I blinked my eyes, stared at my plate, and noticed my fork. An overwhelming fear of touching metal returned. I whispered, "Can I have a plastic fork?"

Momma didn't ask any questions. She opened a drawer and fished around before pushing a plastic fork across the counter. Apparently, whatever I had just been through didn't matter. Nothing more was said about it, and I never went to the doctor to get checked out. It was as if it never happened.

A Moment of Grace

My sister and I are very different in many ways. I wanted affection from her, and she couldn't give it. I did everything she told me to do because I desperately wanted to be loved by her. Now I know that she has always loved me in her highest and best way. She even hugs me now.

The Golden Boy, or Not!

The last day I lived in the house on 23rd Avenue was also the day Ethan was born. I remember things being boxed up and Maw Maw being around a lot. On moving day, we went to Maw Maw and Paw Paw's house to get out of the way of the hustle and bustle. I remember feeling unsettled—Momma wasn't with us, and the son Daddy had been waiting his whole life for had finally arrived. What did it all mean?

Of course, as with most families, the baby got all the attention. I remember feeling jealous of the time Momma's focus and attention was on another child. Though Polly and I had asked for a sister, we got a brother, and he would be staying. I was clearly afraid of how this would affect my position in the family. I had been the baby, and now I would be the middle child. Though I didn't know it at the time, this new pecking order would not be in my favor.

Polly had been born with some serious physical challenges and required a lot of attention. My new baby brother was the "Golden Boy," the heir to the Noble throne who could carry on Daddy's legacy. I was the kid that Momma had been angry with since conception and had wanted out of the house. Being a loving big sister to a new baby brother seemed to be a setup from the beginning. Much to my surprise, the Golden Boy did not live a golden life.

Ethan never got the attention from Daddy that I assumed he would. Daddy had wanted him, but rarely spent one-on-one time with him. Once, when Ethan was 13, he asked Daddy to teach him how to pitch a baseball. Daddy went outside, set up a board with a square, told him the square was his strike zone, and then went back inside to watch sports on TV.

Polly and I were never able to step up and fill in the gaps for attention that Ethan deserved. We girls were used to hanging together and amusing ourselves because Daddy worked all the time and Momma didn't want to be bothered during her soap operas. We would play with him, but we easily bored of him and his little kid toys. Polly was nine and I was eight, and we were all about Barbies and our modern-looking Barbie house. Modern but not particularly sturdy. The house would wobble and tumble all the time, even without Ethan's help. But when Ethan was around, with his not-yet-refined motor skills, it was a recipe for disaster.

The only time Polly and I truly loved playing with Ethan was when he was six years old and we would pretend that he was our sister. We dolled him up in a dress and headband and called him "Stephanie." We were having great fun until Daddy saw us and said, "Take that boy out of those clothes."

"We're just playing," I said. "This is our sister Stephanie!"

"That is not how you play!" my dad said, with a finality that was very clear.

I felt my face flush and shame overtake me, but I didn't know why. Clearly we had done something wrong; I just couldn't figure out what it was. My takeaway was that Ethan couldn't be in a dress. It would become clear as I got older that it was deeper than that, and homophobia was alive and rampant in the family I was born into.

This next memory is very difficult to talk about. I am horrified to remember it and know that I am fully responsible. Many of my dark nights of the soul have included this memory, as I beat myself up and wonder how God could ever love me.

Polly and I were playing with our Barbies in our bedroom and had made sure to lock the door so that Ethan couldn't come in and destroy our Barbie house. He instead decided to creep outside and peer into our window to see what we were doing by putting his hands on the ledge of the bedroom window and pulling himself up to the screen. Pretty athletic actually! When he did that, he was very close to the screen, and when I saw him I reacted without thinking. I picked up a bottle of hairspray from the dresser, went up to the window, and sprayed him in the face. I was joking around and thought it would just scare him off. Within a second, Ethan began screaming and ran back into the house. The spray had gotten into his eyes through the window screen. As I heard Ethan screaming, I felt my knees weaken and my stomach flip. I knew I would be in big trouble! Once my parents realized what had happened, I heard my name being screamed out.

"Michele Ann, get out here!"

In our house, anytime your given name was used, you knew it was serious. When your full given name was used, you were in the biggest trouble of all. I can't remember the exact words that were used, but the essence of my wrongness was boiled down to my unworthiness. I was left with the knowledge that I was the worst sister ever and that my actions were mean and hateful.

"You may have blinded your brother!" Daddy yelled. "How do you feel about your decision now?"

Oh my God, I thought. *If I have blinded my brother, my defenseless little baby brother, I will die. I should die. I am an evil and horrible person.*

The look on my parents' faces had such disappointment and disgust that I believed I most certainly was a deplorable piece of shit. Momma made sure to remind me of how much she and her own brothers had always loved and cared for each other, and I remember her asking, "Why can't you be more like we were?"

I, of course, felt the shame of what I had done to my brother and was very upset with myself. I tried to tell my brother I was sorry, but he ran away from me.

My parents used guilt to get us to do, in their opinion, the right thing. Guilt and shame would often guide me as I put aside my own needs and started holding myself to a ridiculously high standard. I was never given grace, and I never learned to give myself grace for my age, my lack of knowledge, or my lack of experience.

Even today, when I speak with Ethan about our childhood, he clearly remembers that we did not always want him around. It hurts my heart that he also felt abandoned by his big sisters, sisters who should have been there to help him feel loved. I know now why we didn't and couldn't always be there for him, yet I still hate that I hurt him and for a long time wasn't sure how I could redeem myself.

My brother and I hit a rough patch about 17 years ago. After initially being supportive of my wife and me, his religious views came into conflict with my homosexuality. It was a very painful time, and I wasn't allowed to see my nieces and nephew for seven years. Then, one Christmas morning, when he knew I would be at Momma's house, Ethan showed up unannounced. He hugged me and, for him, that was that. I wanted to process what had changed, but he didn't feel we needed to. I am just grateful that we are back in a relationship with one another.

A Moment of Grace

I made many bad decisions as a child, as many of us do. I accept that this is normal. I still feel such pain when I look back because I love my brother so very much. My parents reacted out of fear, and I understand that. I forgive myself, and I forgive them.

North Marries South!

When Momma and Daddy received premarital counseling, the minister joked that he didn't think he could marry my parents because they were like an interracial couple. My parents were confused and shocked, and then he smiled and said, "I don't think your marriage will last because, Bucky, you are from the South, and Carol, you are from the Northern Midwest! You have too many differences!"

My parents met during Daddy's junior year of college and, despite all their differences, were inseparable. They got married during Daddy's senior year in a very intimate ceremony and lived with Grandma and Grandpa for a while. Momma became pregnant, and my older sister was born while Daddy was still in his senior year of college. Even with that big change, it was all doable because Momma had Grandma for support.

After Daddy finished college, my parents moved to North Carolina so Daddy could take a teaching job. That is when everything changed. They had to come to terms with how they would raise a family without the extended support of Momma's family. Momma became an at-home mom, and Daddy's meager 1958 schoolteacher salary didn't afford us the luxury of paying for daycare. We were poor. There were times when Momma wouldn't eat just so she could make sure there was enough food for the rest of us, and there was never money left over for anything other than paying bills. The isolation took its toll on Momma, who was consumed with grief after having to leave her family. The expectations put on her to be more like Daddy's mom, coupled with the exhaustion of raising two young children, made things extremely difficult for her.

Momma and Daddy's marriage to each other was a quintessential 1950s traditional one. Daddy brought home a paycheck and did the outside chores, while Momma did all the cooking, cleaning, laundry, and childcare. Momma waited on Daddy, fixing his food, bringing it to him on a tray, clearing it for him when he was finished, and then bringing him his coffee. What she did for Daddy may have been out of love, and equally because that was the expectation of that era. I asked her about it one time and she simply stated, "That is what wives do; that is how I was raised."

The only thing that may have been uncommon for that era was that Momma had control over the finances. Daddy switched jobs, from Granite Falls High School to Southwest Caldwell High School. Caldwell was bigger, and Daddy would have more opportunities to coach men's basketball at a higher division.

For Momma to use the car during the day, Daddy began carpooling to work with a friend named Laura. As far as I knew, everything seemed fine with this arrangement, but I also observed that Momma and Daddy's relationship was changing. One night, I noticed that Momma hadn't made supper for Daddy, who came up to the kitchen from the downstairs den and made his own sandwich. I thought, *Oh my God, they are going to get a divorce!* It was just the strangest thing. They weren't talking, and Daddy had made his own food. They made snippy comments to each other from time to time, but they never fought or cursed one another in our presence. I couldn't figure it out ... until Momma confided in me that she thought Daddy was having an affair.

I believe that Momma and I were both so traumatized by what comes next that we have successfully buffered our memories for our protection. To the best of my knowledge, I was in middle school. Whenever I have tried to clarify my age when this happened, Momma's go-to answer has been, "I didn't know that happened" or "I don't remember." To the best of our recollection, this is how it went.

Momma gave her evidence that Daddy and Laura were having an affair: They would stop talking when Momma came into the room, and when they would all sit on the couch, Momma would be in the middle and Daddy and Laura would put their arms up behind Momma; once, when Momma turned around, she caught them touching hands. She said that of course they had tried to come up with excuses and explanations, but that made her even angrier because they would not come out and tell the truth about what she had seen.

I didn't know what to think. I loved Daddy, and I had also been Momma's loyal confidant for so long that I felt I should believe her. At one point Momma even questioned me, "Do you think I'm lying? Are you calling me a liar?"

"No, Momma," I said. "I don't think that." And with those words I had just taken a side, one that was against Daddy.

I felt as if a brick had just been dropped into my stomach, and my breath got shallow. I couldn't bear taking sides! I didn't want to go against Momma because I had seen her wrath and I didn't want her to be mad at me! I already felt that if I did something against her wishes she would withhold her love from me. The love in my house always felt very conditional.

I didn't know what to do about it either. Was I supposed to fix it? Was I supposed to pray to God to make it go away? Momma always relied on me to pray and tell God what to do because I had talked about being a missionary and liked going to church. Momma didn't tell me to pray, and I didn't know how to pray about this because I didn't know what to think about it. I wished that Momma would just tell me what I was supposed to do! I learned that day to be careful what I wished for.

It was a few weeks later when Momma told me she needed to go to Illinois. Grandma, who had suffered two major strokes, was going to have surgery, and the outcome could be fatal. Momma and Daddy had talked about it and decided we couldn't all afford to go, even though Daddy was on summer break from his teaching duties. Momma strongly felt she needed to be there, and Daddy had agreed.

Around this same time, I heard Momma and Daddy having an argument. Without school to go to, Daddy decided to wash the rug in our living room. Laura offered to help, and Momma was very angry about this.

"She doesn't need to be in my house while I am gone," Momma asserted.

Daddy responded, "I think it is very nice of her to offer to help while you're gone."

Momma countered this with, "I don't think you need her here; the rug is not that big. And what is she going to do, just stand around and watch you work? Why does she need to do that?"

Momma was also upset about what would happen when we went to the community pool while she was gone. My parents had found a way to pay for a summer pass to the pool, and to get the most out of our tickets, we would go swimming every day. Momma knew that Laura would also be there. The year before, our two families had both gotten summer passes and had gone to the pool together. Following the argument about the rug, I was called into Momma's room.

"While I am gone," she said, "you cannot leave Daddy and Laura in the same room together. No matter what they tell you, stay in the room with them while Daddy is shampooing the carpet. Keep your eyes on them at all times."

I felt like the floor had become a merry-go-round; my mind was spinning as I tried to take in this request and deal with all the feelings that came up for me. Panic set in and I could feel my heart pounding in my chest. *She wants me to spy and tell on Daddy? What if Daddy found out? What would he do to me? What if I can't do it?* I felt like I was going to faint!

As if that weren't enough, her next set of instructions were worse: "You will be going to the pool. You need to sit near them and listen to what they are talking about. Also, I need you to find out if your daddy and Laura are having an affair."

WHAT?! I screamed inside my head. I couldn't get the words out at the time, but I was scared to death about what I had just been asked to do.

Momma continued, "When you are at the pool one day, get Laura alone and ask her if she is having an affair with Daddy. You ask her. I need this done before I come home."

I could feel the color drain from my face and was at a loss for words. All I could think of was how mad Daddy was going to be if he found out I did this. I didn't know what Laura would do. Would she get angry with me and tell on me? I would certainly be in trouble with Daddy if that happened. The sad thing was, Laura had befriended me and believed in me. I felt we were friends. Momma had babysat Laura's daughter, Kelly, before she was able to attend kindergarten, and Kelly had become like a little sister to us. I just didn't know how I was going to do it.

Trying to reason with Momma, I said, "Momma, Daddy will get really mad, and I don't know how to get Laura alone. I just don't think I can do it!"

"You have to do this!" Momma continued. "I will expect it to be done before I get back. You have a week."

I stood there frozen as Momma left the room. I felt like my feet were glued to the floor. Momma's voice yelling for me to come do some chore jarred me back to reality. I stuffed all those feelings down into the pit of my stomach, as far as they would go, and went to do my chore.

Momma left, Daddy started the rug project, and, of course, Laura was there to help. I was hanging out and watching, as instructed. My brother and sister were out playing in the neighborhood, and when Daddy told me to go out and play, I gave him the excuse that I wanted to help. When Daddy kept asking me to go get things, I would run to get whatever it was while my heart pounded; I feared that something would happen before I got back to the living room and that I would have to tell Momma I had failed at my job. This went on for hours.

Then came our pool day. I knew that it was coming, and I was sick to my stomach. I couldn't figure out how I was going to do it.

Daddy and Laura sunned themselves at the same time and then cooled off in the water at the same time. I sat near them, sunning and cooling myself off whenever they did. Daddy must have picked up on the change in my behavior at the pool, because normally they couldn't get me out of the water. He said, "Get in the water; that's what we're here for."

"I thought I'd work on my tan," I said.

"You don't need a tan. Get in the water and go swim like you usually do."

He was right; I was like a fish in the water and would usually swim all day long whenever we were at the pool. But on this day, I had barely been in the water at all, except to cool off.

To avoid getting into trouble and looking too suspicious, I got in the water and splashed around, doing my best to listen to their conversations while pretending to swim—as close to them as I could. I kept trying to get up the courage to ask the big question.

Finally, I asked Laura if I could talk to her about something and she joined me in the shallow end of the pool. I felt as if I had stopped breathing, and I couldn't get the words to come out. I could see my dad looking in our direction, and that just made things worse. I held my face down so he couldn't see my lips.

Eventually Laura said, "You can talk to me."

So I just blurted it out: "Momma told me to ask you if you're having an affair with Daddy."

She immediately denied it.

"Okay, I'm sorry," I said.

She got up and went back to sit with my dad. I couldn't even look at her and was too scared to look at him, as I imagined that he was going to thrash across the pool and whip me right there. Thankfully, that didn't happen. As a matter of fact, I can't remember anything after that, including whether he said anything to me about it or not.

The trauma of betraying my dad, possibly killing any relationship I had with Laura, and having absolutely no one to talk to about it almost broke me emotionally. I do recall the ride home was very quiet and seemed excruciatingly long.

When I got home, I comforted myself with my favorite stress reliever: sugar. It really didn't matter what form the sugar came in, though I did tend to gravitate toward milk chocolate. Worst case scenario, if nothing else was available, I would just eat spoonful after spoonful of sugar straight from the bowl.

Momma had unknowingly enabled this addiction by separating bags of candy into three, same-sized peanut butter jars. Each jar was labeled with our names and placed in a lower cabinet, in birth order—of course. We were given a weekly allowance of candy in our jar and could eat it whenever we wanted. If we ate it all in one day, we went the rest of the week without candy, or so the rule was. I often would go through my jar within a day or two, and I would also often get caught eating out of my sister's or brother's candy jar after having gone through all of mine. Feeding my feelings was the only way to comfort the overwhelming emotions that were pent up inside of me.

When Momma came back home that weekend, she grilled me about every detail of the goings on while she had been away. What did they do? What did they say? Where did they sit? All these questions. Momma wasn't happy with my answers because I couldn't give her a detailed account of what Daddy and Laura had said to each other since they wouldn't talk when I was in the room. I told Momma I had tried to hold my breath and strained to listen to their conversations, but that was of no use. I knew that if I told Momma that Daddy had forced me to get in the water instead of spending the day sitting near them at the pool, it would seem like more evidence against Daddy. Maybe I should have told her, but what if they were just friends? I was still holding out hope that Daddy and Laura were not having an affair.

Things between Momma and Daddy were very awkward after that. They just never fully recovered. After many tense years, our family and Laura's family stopped socializing completely.

Daddy retired in 1989. Momma got cancer in 1993. It was just Daddy, Momma, and breast cancer. Once again, I was told to pray. Momma, being very aware of her looks, feared that she would lose her hair. Soon after her diagnosis, she had a wig made to match her natural hair color.

Momma wound up having a mastectomy. She came home from the hospital with drainage tubes attached to her body, which Daddy had to strip for her by squeezing the liquid out of them. Though he was trying to help, his strength was overwhelming for the fragile state that Momma's body was in. She was in pain, and he was scared to hurt her even more. When Momma could no longer take the pain of having Daddy strip the tubes and couldn't wait for someone else to come do it for her, she ended up stripping the tubes herself. She was given a low dose of chemotherapy just to be sure that if anything else was lingering, the medicine would take care of it.

The dynamics shifted between them during that time. Momma still took care of the finances, but Daddy had to step up and do some things that Momma couldn't do. He would take care of the heavy laundry and do the vacuuming and dusting while Momma recovered from post-surgery drains and weightlifting limits. He would also drive her to doctor's appointments, both because she was not yet able to drive and so he could be aware of how she was doing and what he needed to do to help her. Daddy also started going to church with her, instead of using his old "Sunday migraine" excuse.

Then, after years of smoking, Daddy started having more breathing issues. Smoking, like drinking, had started in the Navy for Daddy, and he smoked most of his life. He told Momma years before that he had stopped smoking, and he had—at the house. But it seems he was still smoking during his carpool trips to school with Laura, who let him bum cigarettes off her. He would smoke in the teacher's lounge and come home smelling of smoke, telling Momma that all the other teachers smoked in the lounge and that she must just be smelling their smoke on him.

About a year after he "stopped smoking," Daddy suffered a lung collapse, which forced him to confess that he hadn't really stopped. A tube was inserted into his chest after he was officially diagnosed with emphysema. He started on a portable oxygen cart, and later he required a full-time oxygen concentrator. The 30 foot oxygen tubing allowed him to walk from the kitchen to the bedroom and bathroom. He could still travel, but it was a struggle, and he didn't like being in public with his oxygen cart.

Toward the end, he struggled with his ability to make simple movements, and he would go days without bathing because the walk across the hallway from the bedroom to the bathroom was too exhausting. When he did bathe, Momma had to hold his arms up for him and wash him because he didn't have the strength to raise his own arms and hold them up. Daddy was mortified that Momma had to bathe him. He was embarrassed that, after being so athletic throughout his entire life, he couldn't even hold up his arms. Momma remembers that his skin got scaly in between baths, and he would sometimes go weeks without bathing.

Daddy got progressively worse, and there were times he would have Momma take him to the emergency room for urgent care. He would return home but was never much better. This was not an illness that would ever get better.

I got the call on February 4th, 1998, from by brother, Ethan. I was just about to take a shower before getting ready for work.

"Daddy has been rushed to the hospital by ambulance this time, and it doesn't look good."

"Does Polly know?" I asked.

"Yes," he said, "I called her too."

Right after that, my sister Polly called.

"I'm heading your way," she said. "Do you want to ride together?"

"Sure. I'll jump in the shower and be out by the time you get here."

Before I could even walk away from the phone, it rang again.

"Hello?" I answered.

There was silence, and then Ethan tearfully said, "He's gone."

"He's dead?! What happened?!"

"I'm not sure. Momma just said he died in the emergency room. I don't think she has talked with a doctor."

I then called Polly who said, "Ethan called me just a minute ago. I'll be there soon. I guess we don't have to rush."

I turned on the hot water in the shower, got in, and cried.

While I was packing a few things, Polly arrived, and we headed to Hickory. On the way, I started coughing.

"Are you sick?" Polly asked.

"I wasn't yesterday," I said. "I worked out at the gym for over an hour!"

I coughed again.

"Well, you sound sick now!" Polly said.

"Hey, you know how people get grief-related illnesses after someone dies?"

"Yeah."

"Well," I coughed, "I must be academically gifted in grief, because Daddy just died and I'm already sick!" (Go ahead and moan; our family has the weirdest sense of humor!)

When we got to the hospital, Momma was still in the lobby. She told us, "Daddy was in a room surrounded by ER doctors. I waved to him through the window of the door, and he waved back. I couldn't stay there and was walking down the hall to wait in the lobby. The ER doctor said that within seconds, Daddy had a massive heart attack and died."

Momma looked up at us before she continued, "All those ER doctors standing around him, and he dies, and they can't do anything about it."

Gathering our thoughts, we planned to get Momma home and then contact the funeral home. We went as a family to pick out the coffin and prepare for the service. Momma made lists of who to contact, including family, ball players, the church, and friends.

The next few days were a fog as we moved around one another to get things done. I continued to cough throughout the funeral home visit, the viewing, the funeral, and the very damp, cold, and rainy graveside service. As the weekend ended, it was becoming clearer that my "academically gifted grief response" might just be something more. I would find out later that I had whooping cough.

Momma has never wanted another relationship. She says that it is exhausting and scary to be a caretaker. She would rush home from church or choir practice, always fearful that she might walk in and find Daddy dead. She said that she truly loves living alone, but she is sometimes lonely. She eats when and what she wants, she cleans or doesn't clean when she wants, and she never has to consider anybody else's needs but her own. She has finally found her perfect niche.

A Moment of Grace

My parents loved each other. Their love evolved over time, and they chose to remain together. They were comfortable in their roles, never really knowing anything different. Daddy became very compassionate throughout Momma's cancer journey and, although he didn't continue, he did go to church more regularly while Momma was battling the disease. Momma still gets angry at the years she believes Daddy had an affair, and she still grieves the death of her husband.

Do not judge me by my successes;
judge me by how many times
I fell down and got back up again.

—**NELSON MANDELA**

Trials

Part 2

Jesus Facade

At the beginning of high school in 1973, I was full-blown into cementing my place in God's kingdom. I became president of the church's youth group, would attend church religiously every Sunday, and even preached a sermon on Youth Sunday. Per my earlier faith journey, I was committed to being a missionary and walking the dusty roads of Damascus. But at this point, although I didn't consciously dwell on my fear of unworthiness, I had assumed this persona as my truth. I didn't focus on doubts or my questions of who made God. I put on the "Jesus Facade" and lived each day performing my Christian duties.

Though I didn't call myself a "Jesus freak," looking back at pictures I realize I might have been perceived that way. I believed I was a Christian and that I was expected to look and act like one, so I wore my "Jesus Is Coming" button to school and carried my Bible. I started a group at school during study hour, during which we read and discussed the Bible, and I prayed before meals and showed everyone that I was a Christian. I must have ignored Jesus's teachings about self-righteous people.

One morning, I was scheduled to do the morning devotions over the loudspeaker (there was no separation of church and state in North Carolina in those days). Unfortunately, our school was vandalized the night before I was supposed to give the morning devotion. As we arrived that morning, we saw our lockers had been dumped into the halls and the front office was in complete chaos. I was abruptly told that morning that devotions were canceled. Though I advocated that this was the absolute best time to address the students and pray, I was outvoted.

Without any notice or discussion, morning devotions never happened again, the little group of Bible misfits disbanded from lack of interest, and I was back to walking through the halls with my "Jesus Is Coming" button and my Bible.

I always attended our Advent Christian-supported summer camp and met many of the choir members from our church-supported Berkshire Christian College. I had decided years ago that I would attend this school and dreamed of being one of the choir members. All through high school I talked about going to Berkshire to study missions; subconsciously, I still desperately wanted God's approval.

My parents were not amused by my staunch desire to go to Berkshire, however. They were driven by location and finances and couldn't imagine me being in Massachusetts at a private college, so they encouraged me to apply to Appalachian State University (ASU) to become a teacher. I once wanted to be a teacher and thought that if my dad and I shared that in common, I would get his approval. However, by the time I got to high school, I was more motivated by God's approval.

Though I desperately wanted to pursue a writing career when I entered college, that goal was also shot down by my parents. They gave nothing in the form of praise for my writing skills and convinced me that I couldn't make money as a writer. No matter what I wrote, their comments were always something like, "That was good Midge, but …" Such critiques shut down my flow of creativity.

Much to my parents' dismay, I ended up applying only to Berkshire Christian College. My SAT scores were not high enough for the University of North Carolina at Chapel Hill, which was never really a goal of mine, though I did love the Tar Heels! I probably could have gotten into ASU, but since I didn't want to go there, there was no point in applying. I did get accepted to Berkshire Christian, though, and I was so excited—though no one else was.

I finished suffering through my four years of high school, a place that, although I was voted "Most Dependable," was not a happy one for me. I did well with my teachers, was a very good student, and was helpful to others. But though I could talk to all the cliques, I was never a part of any. My parents were very strict and didn't allow us to go to parties or ball games, so that didn't give me much of a chance to socialize or get to know people outside of classes. I went to junior prom with a group of girls who didn't have dates. For senior prom, a boy that liked my sister agreed to take me. I think he really just wanted to see Polly, but he was very nice and kind. He even wiped off his car seats so my dress, which my aunt had handmade, wouldn't get dirty.

By the time graduation came around, I was ready. I wanted desperately to leave Hickory; I wanted to be in New England and start a new life.

That new life started a week after graduation. To test my calling and prove to my parents that this was my purpose, I decided to join a mission trip to India. Obviously, this was not a popular decision among the rest of the family. Without the support of my parents, I went full steam ahead—with all my eggs in one basket!

A Moment of Grace

I understand now that my parents were only trying to give me honest feedback and that they didn't intend to purposely hurt me.

9
Testing the Call

During my senior year of high school, I heard about a mission trip to India with Teen Missions International, and I signed up for it. The mission was to build a church in the small village of Palavakkam, where our missionaries were stationed. At that time, they were worshiping in a thatch-roofed hut that leaked every time it rained, so they needed help rebuilding it. Each mission team member would ask for sponsorships of $60 to cover the cost of their plane tickets to and from their stay at the Lord's Boot Camp, the training facility in Merritt Island, Florida. The team would be there for two weeks while learning how to build a church from the ground up as well as how to evangelize. They would also get to engage in a Marine obstacle course as a team-building activity. Following these two weeks, if team members accepted the call at their candlelight commitment ceremony, they would be on their way to India.

I could feel that tug in my soul—*I must do this!*

When I excitedly told my parents that I had learned about an awesome opportunity and was just starting to tell them about the trip, my Daddy interrupted and gave me a resounding, "No."

"Why not?" I pleaded. "I haven't even told you how it's all going to work out."

"You have already been accepted to college, and there is no reason to do this. You need to stay here and get a job to earn money."

"But there are people who will sponsor me, so it won't cost me anything to go."

"Oh, is that what you think? I said no and that's it."

I knew that look on his face. That was his final answer, and no amount of pleading would work. Momma just watched and didn't say a word. I felt heartbroken. I already knew I had to go, and I wanted to go, and I couldn't believe he wouldn't allow it. I should have known he wouldn't approve because he never agreed to anything that would cost money. He had already been upset that I was planning to attend an out-of-state college.

For months, at every youth group meeting, the leaders would talk about the trip and encourage us to sign up. As the deadline was nearing, I was getting nervous. I talked to Momma about it, saying, "It's really a way to test my calling."

"Your daddy said no, and he won't change his mind," she insisted.

I felt my heart sink. I felt hopeless. Then I got mad. *How dare he turn me down on this? We never get to do anything, and this is important. I should just go anyway!* Then I stopped and thought, *Yeah right, like that would fly.* I just couldn't figure out a way to make this happen.

A few weeks later, I went to another youth group meeting where the India trip came up again. The excitement returned and I signed up.

"Great, Midge!" my youth leader said. "I think this is a perfect fit for you! Your parents will be so proud."

"Probably not," I said. "They don't know I'm signing up, but I really feel like I have to do this."

"If you are called to this, I'm sure they will understand," she assured.

"Let's hope so."

"Just make sure you tell them. You don't want them finding out from someone else."

"Yes, that would be bad."

I felt exhilarated when I put my name on the list, but as the meeting went on, anxiety began to creep up in me and I started worrying about how mad Daddy would be when he found out.

I was so anxious heading home that evening. Walking into the house, all my breath left my body the moment I saw my dad standing in the kitchen.

"Guess what?" I asked.

"What?"

"I really feel that God wants me to go on this India trip, so I signed up."

The look on my dad's face pierced my heart, and I felt the color drain from my body.

"You did what? I specifically told you that you were not going. You better take your name off that list."

"Daddy, I know, and I'm sorry to go against what you said, but I am 18, and this is really important, and I know I can get the scholarships and it won't cost us anything."

"Well, okay, smarty pants. If you think that people during this recession are going to fork out money so you can go to India, then good luck. You will not get any money from us."

"Really? I can go?"

Daddy glared at me. "If you can get the money, you can go, but that's not going to happen."

I felt pure adrenalin-filled excitement, but I also felt like crap in the pit of my stomach. I had never, ever blatantly gone against Daddy's decisions. I was also scared that he might be right that no one would sponsor me.

The next week I received information about the team I would be on and its leaders, the scholarship cards, a tape to learn Tamil (the Indian dialect spoken in Madras), suggestions on how and where to ask for sponsorships, and the items I needed for the trip. My heart sank reading the list: I was going to need many immunizations against malaria and other illnesses, a passport, a duffle bag, boots, work clothes, and many other items that I hadn't planned on buying. I could just hear my dad saying, "You won't get any money from us."

Over the next few months, I presented at churches, women's groups, and the Rotary Club, making my case and explaining my desire to be a missionary. I explained that this trip would help me test that calling and that our work team would build a church in India for the people of Palavakkam who desperately needed to replace the small grass hut they used for worship. I talked about the Lord's Boot Camp and how that experience would help our team bond and learn how to get the work done together. At the end of each presentation, I ended with a Q&A session and encouraged people to come to me afterward to ask any other questions they may not have had a chance to ask.

I received sponsorships at every presentation. Some people were able to give at the full sponsorship level of $60, and those who couldn't still gave me $5, $10, or $20 and told me to use the money to buy whatever I needed. It was a warm and humbling feeling to be supported and to know that all the people who attended these talks were very enthusiastic about this mission trip and trusted me to go and do what I said I would.

My parents came to these presentations, and I heard people say to Daddy, "I bet you are so proud of Midge for going on a mission trip."

"Yes, I am," he would say. He still hadn't talked to me much since the night he found out I signed up, and I thought that was super hypocritical.

Throughout my childhood, I learned that love was conditional: agree with me and I will talk with you; go against me and I will withdraw from you. Trust and emotional abandonment issues still rear their ugly little heads from time to time.

A few weeks before the deadline to send my sponsorships to Teen Missions International, I totaled all the money. I had done it! I had all the money I needed to make the trip. I even had $500 in cash from those sweet little ladies who gave me permission to use it for whatever I needed (which came in handy for buying items I hadn't known I would need). I was going to India via the Lord's Boot Camp in Florida. But first, I had an untimely gift to manage.

A Moment of Grace

I was so angry that my parents would not honor my calling. Would I want my 18-year-old to fly halfway around the world? Absolutely not! I understand their concerns yet remain sad that they weren't able to be excited or supportive of my journey.

10

The Slough of Despond

All calls are met with some trials. Mine came two weeks before I was supposed to leave for my mission: my period began for the first time since being struck by lightning when I was 12 years old. I didn't know it then, but it would last the entire time I was in Florida and India. Some say God has a sense of humor, but I was *not* laughing!

I met up with my North Carolina team members from our denomination at one of the local churches. With plenty of monthly provisions packed, we stowed our gear in the van and took off with hugs, good wishes, tears, and cheers. Momma and Daddy were not as enthusiastic as the other parents in their send-off.

The plan was to travel to a Jerry's Union 76 truck stop located halfway between North Carolina and Florida, but we missed our connection and spent two days in the noisy parking lot in a cramped van. When the transport finally picked us up and dropped us off at the Lord's Boot Camp, we were instructed to get our heavy duffle bags and walk down a footpath to our tent site. The footpath trail was one-and-a-half miles long, and the Florida morning was misty and humid. I could hear swishing sounds coming from the tall grass beside the footpath. My anxiety beginning to rise, I thought for the first time since signing my name on that paper, *What have I done? I'm not sure I can do this!*

We arrived at our tents, and I couldn't wait to finally stretch out and get some sleep. An adult male walked up to me and asked, "Are you the North Carolina kids?"

"Yes," I spoke up. "We haven't slept in two days. Is there somewhere we can dump our gear and get some sleep?"

He looked at me as if I had two heads. "You're part of this team. We have KP this morning. Dump your gear in those tents, get in line, and get back up to the mess tent for instructions." KP, I learned, was kitchen patrol. Our team would be serving breakfast to all the other teams.

"Is he kidding me?" I said to my buddy Sam.

"I don't guess so," said Sam. "We'd better get in line."

We dumped our gear and got into the line of teammates who were sleepily walking back up the long path that our team had just walked down. I was already sweating and itching in my cheap nylon polo shirt, and I was still thinking, *What have I done? I don't think I can handle this!*

After breakfast I asked if we could rest. The leader looked me square in the eye and said, "We have the obstacle course. If you want to be on this team, you have to do what the team does. Get in line and get ready to set a good pace. This is a timed event."

This "timed event," as he called it, was an obstacle course set up by the Marines and was supposed to build team cohesiveness. We would tiptoe our work boots through tires, run a mile through the jungle, grab a rope and swing over a moat (named the Slough of Despond), climb up and down a 30-foot rope ladder, dive through hanging tires, and then get over a 12-foot wall.

The leader screamed, "GET IN LINE NOW!"

I turned back to Sam and said, "He can make us run, but he can't make us be first or be fast."

THE SLOUGH OF DESPOND

Sam laughed and we both headed to the back of the line.

Our team members were all lined up and off we went. Sam and I trotted down the path as our leader screamed behind us, "Faster, let's go!"

Sam and I, running side by side, looked at each other as we ran around a palm tree when, all of a sudden, Sam was gone! I stopped running and looked back to see Sam lying in the sand face down, then laughing as he rolled himself over. I started laughing too as I went back to him and exclaimed, "Sam, what happened? Oh my God, you're bleeding!"

We were both in stupid brain laughter at that point. "I know," he laughed. "I ran into the palm frond."

"Keep running!" the leader yelled as he came up behind us. "What are you doing? Get up and keep running!"

"He's bleeding!" I half-screamed/half-laughed.

"Get up. You're fine."

I grabbed hold of Sam and pulled him up. "Do you need a doctor?"

"No," laughed Sam.

"Let's go!" yelled the leader.

Sam and I took off down the path and into the jungle. We laughed, ran, tripped over roots, and finally emerged from the jungle to face the Slough of Despond.[2] This obstacle was a massive pit full of gray, muddy, mucky water with ropes hanging over it. The first person to get to the moat had to propel themselves through the air, grab the rope, and then toss it to the next teammate. Sam ran ahead as I inhaled deeply to get air to come back into my lungs. He grabbed the rope that was tossed to

---

[2] The "Slough of Despond" is part of Teen Missions International's training obstacle course that involves jumping onto a rope and swinging over a muddy pool of water. Its relevance comes from a fictional deep bog in John Bunyan's novel *The Pilgrim's Progress*, in which the protagonist Christian sinks under the weight of his guilt about his sins; *Encyclopaedia Britannica Online*, s.v. "The Pilgrim's Progress," accessed April 2, 2023, https://www.britannica.com/topic/The-Pilgrims-Progress.

him and swung, as the Tarzan call reverberated out of his vocal cords. I made it to the side of the moat and caught the rope as he swung it back to me.

"NO WAY!" I called to him.

"Midge, you have to!"

I looked across the massive pit. "No, I can't," I said.

"JUMP!" I heard from behind me. Three guesses as to who was yelling.

I looked back at Sam who said, "Jump! You can do it!" as the leader closing in on me screamed again, "JUMP!"

I jumped … and I am not sure what happened. I don't know whether I fell asleep or passed out from fear or fatigue, because I can't remember anything after I jumped—until I heard Sam scream my name the moment my face hit the wall on the other side of the moat. I landed in the mucky gray water with a woozy head and no idea what other injuries I had. As I turned to walk out of the water, several people screamed for me to stop and grabbed for my arms. I lifted my arms, and they dragged me over the side of the moat. Several people asked if I was okay, and Sam was hovering—until the leader yelled, "KEEP GOING! We are not done!"

"Sorry, Midge," Sam said as he took off for the next obstacle.

I stood off to the side, realizing that my four bottom teeth were loose and my mouth was bleeding. While I tried to spit out the mud and blood in my mouth without spitting out my teeth, the leader came over and said, "You have to keep going or I will have to take you to the nurse!"

"Well," I said, holding my finger in front of my bottom teeth, "that's probably a good idea!"

As he led me to a trailer, I felt like I was taking a walk of shame. He then placed me in the direct sunshine, behind a line of other kids who had also been injured on the obstacle course. I stood there for several minutes until the door finally opened. The nurse looked down the line, rested her eyes on me, pointed, and said, "You, yes you, come on. You're next."

Passing by many other kids, I walked up the rickety steps to the air-conditioned trailer. The cool air immediately made me feel better, but then I had to try to answer questions while tasting dirt and blood and trying to keep my teeth in my mouth. The nurse gave me water and a bowl, then left it to me to clean my mouth out the best I could while she went to attend to the ever-growing line of the walking wounded.

When the nurse returned, she placed a fan by me and told me to lie back and rest a while. *Finally!* I thought. *I can sleep.* I felt a twinge of guilt that my North Carolina teammates were not as lucky though.

I am not sure how long I was there lying down, trying not to swallow, and resting in the cool air. When the nurse returned, she said, "I can't keep you much longer. I think you'll be okay. No obstacle course for the rest of the week."

"Shouldn't I go to a dentist?" I asked.

"Oh, once you're at the camp, you're not allowed to leave."

"What? My teeth are falling out! I need a dentist."

"I'm sorry, honey, but I can't send you to a dentist. Just be careful with how you eat over the next few days and they will tighten back up."

She didn't examine my mouth. She didn't look at the four teeth that were hanging on by their wobbly roots or realize that several of my teeth had been chipped, including my front one. For the next few days, the only way I could manage eating was by putting extremely small pieces of food in my mouth and swallowing without chewing. The bright light was that I didn't have to run the obstacle course for a week—but I did have to swim with alligators!

Not running the obstacle course gave my body a chance to heal, but my injury didn't keep me out of the drowning prevention and rescue class. Why we would need this skill in India was a mystery to me, but the next morning we walked down to a swimming hole for class.

As we emerged from the trail, we came to a small body of dark water surrounded by tall grass and other flora. We were instructed on how to make a lifesaving jump into the water so that we could swim out and save a drowning person. When one of the leaders demonstrated, I thought, *No way!*

The point was to jump off the pier with one knee up and both arms outstretched so that upon impact your head stays above water. If done correctly, the drowning person can be sighted without the rescuer losing them by going under the water. As many team members got in line, I kept letting people get in front of me. Eventually, it was my turn.

Oh my God, I thought, *please don't let me drown or get eaten by something.*

I stood on the pier, trembling with nerves. I knew how to swim and loved swimming in a pool, but this was nothing like the pool. Reviewing the steps in my head, I jumped. I hit the water and sank like a ton of bricks, then scrambled to get back to the surface.

"You went under!" bellowed the leader as I swam as fast as I could to the sandbar. "You need to do it again."

"Now?" I hollered back from my safe spot.

"Now would be good."

Begrudgingly, I swam back through the black lagoon. I tried several times, but I couldn't figure out the motion of jumping, so I kept going under water every time!

In week two, we were informed that we wouldn't be going to that class anymore—because an alligator had taken residence there. WAIT … WHAT?! Did the alligator just take up residence? Had it been there all along and we hadn't known, or had they just found it? Once again I thought to myself, *What have I done? This must have been a mistake!*

Though I felt extremely happy that my time in that nasty water was over, I soon learned that I was cleared to return to the obstacle course, which was an anxiety-provoking endeavor. I dreaded the run through the jungle because I knew what was waiting for me. The rest of the team

THE SLOUGH OF DESPOND

was now faster and more proficient, but I had never gotten past the second part—the dreaded Slough of Despond.

The morning of my return to the obstacle course, my faithful pal Sam was there to do the run with me—from the back, of course! The leader reminded me that the team's time included my individual time and encouraged me to run faster because there was a prize for the fastest team. Thank you very much (NOT) for applying more pressure to what I was already feeling!

Sam and I took off. Clearly I wasn't fast enough, because the leader barked his orders to "Run faster!"

We got through the tire run and the jungle run, then came to the Slough of Despond. Just like the first time, Sam jumped off the side of the pit and threw the rope back to me. The leader was shouting, "Jump!" and I could barely breathe. My heart was pounding in my chest.

"I can't do it," I replied.

"Yes you can!" screamed the leader. "Jump! You have to jump!"

Grabbing the rope even tighter, I jumped off, hearing Sam scream, "Pick up your feet!"

My boots skimmed the water as I flew toward the wall. As I got to the other side, Sam grabbed me and pulled me up and over, helping me land on the ground.

"You did it!" Sam screamed.

"Oh my God!" I exclaimed.

Just then, I heard the leader say, "Keep running! You are not finished!"

Next came the 30-foot rope ladder—up, over, and down—then a dive through the tire swing and a climb over the 12-foot wall. By the time I got to the wall, many of my teammates were already over it. I stood there huffing, trying to catch my breath. Two of my male team members were at the bottom of the wall and two were sitting on top of it, the theory being that the guys on the ground would boost others up and the guys at the top would help them over.

I was so out of shape. The guys on the ground propelled me up, and the guys at the top grabbed my hands. "Walk the wall, Midge," they encouraged. I struggled to keep my boots on the wall as they kept sliding. "We got you, Midge. Lean back a little and keep walking." They strained to keep me from falling off the top, as I must have felt like a sack of potatoes. Finally, I made it to the top with cheers from my team.

The leader screamed for me to get off the back of the wall so the guys could finish and our team's final time could be called.

Thinking back, I wonder whether we won the timed event. I highly doubt it. I may not have been fast, but I am not a quitter. I have so much internal strength coming from some survival place in me that even when I want to quit, it doesn't seem to be in my DNA to do so.

The two very long and excruciating weeks in Florida culminated in a commitment ceremony. We had bonded as a team, learned how to do the construction work that would be required on the mission, and finally had our visas come through. At first, Indira Gandhi and the Indian government did not want us to come, then they wanted us to live in the village huts. This wasn't possible, though, because the missionaries required that we live on their compound. There was even talk of bailing on the India trip and going to Haiti to instead build an airstrip (which sounded awful to me!). Thankfully our visas were at last accepted, and the missionaries were permitted to have us live on their compound.

By the day of the commitment ceremony, our mission trip to India was a go. Now we had to decide, individually, if we were willing to go as well. Everyone was given a candle as they entered a circus tent. The tent was filled with all the teams heading out into the world with various missions to complete, such as building churches and other structures, bike evangelism, and puppet ministry. Palpable anxious excitement filled the air.

Since I still had my never-ending period, my parents had arrived to make sure I was okay, and they planned to take me home. One of our other team members, who had been forced by her parents to come, had already left with her family after clearly deciding she couldn't do this. Not wanting this to be me, I talked with my parents about my desire to test this calling and my concern that if I quit, I would let down too many people who had supported me. I told them my period had slowed down alot, and they left the decision up to me.

When the candle was handed to me, instead of passing it on to the next person, I lit it. I was heading to India!

A Moment of Grace

My parents were worried, and rightfully so. I was so proud of them for allowing me to decide, and then giving me the autonomy to stand by that decision. They drove all the way to Florida to bring me home and didn't guilt me into going back with them.

11

The Land of Contrast, Dysentery, and Homesickness

The morning after our commitment ceremony, our team loaded our gear into a school bus that took us to the airport. Each team member carried a 60-pound duffle bag filled with personal items and canned goods. Including the leaders, we were a 45-person team. All of us crammed into a school bus with no air-conditioning, poor shocks, and not-so-cushiony seats made the ride from Florida to New York's LaGuardia Airport that much more hot, squished, and uncomfortable!

Once we got to the airport, we unloaded our gear and traipsed through the lobby in a mass of oddness—attracting a lot of stares and giggles as we walked to our gate. We girls were required to wear dresses along with our combat boots. I was thankful I had brought a floor-length dress, made especially for me by a friend's mom. The boys, of course, were allowed to wear jeans with their boots.

Once we made it to our gate, I felt my nervousness increase. I had never flown in an airplane and my anxiety about that was ramping up. We boarded the plane, I found my seat, stored my carry-on, sat down, buckled up, and tried to breathe. Then I felt a familiar sensation. My period had restarted with full force. I got up from my seat and made my way to the bathroom. I was in the middle of washing off my dress when I started feeling like I was going to pass out. I was hot, everything around me was shaking, and I almost lost my balance. That is when I saw a flashing sign next to the bathroom mirror: Return to Your Seat. Only then did I realize, *OMG, we're taking off!*

I dried off as well as I could, and as I hurried down the aisle I realized we were taxiing down the runway! I quickly got into my seat and buckled up again, and the plane rose off the runway. Though I experienced a deep sense of gratitude for getting back to my seat in time, I also felt a sense of dread. I had had my period for four weeks straight at that point, and now I was flying halfway around the world to a place I had no idea about and my body seemed like it was not in my control.

Looking back now, I realize that during my younger years there was very little faith being practiced on my part. Every part of my life to this point had been part of my need to be loved by God, to prove myself in the things I did, and to do things myself without relying on others to do them for me. Instead of prayerfully talking to God about what I was going through, I spent my time exclaiming "OMG" when things went wrong. But I was about to face the most challenging time of my life. Old issues would return—homesickness, resentment, unworthiness—and India would become my training ground for a lifetime of seeking what I wanted to find. I wanted a relationship with God that was authentic. I didn't want it to be based on proving myself but on knowing that God loved me and that I was important to God without having to prove it.

Our flight landed in Rome where we had a day and a half layover. We toured the Colosseum, explored the streets of the city, and shopped! When I was finally able to shower and get myself clean, I began to feel a bit more human.

Landing in New Delhi was very different from landing in Rome. The airport was hot and muggy, and there were lizards crawling on the walls. Armed guards were standing on platforms above the lobby. We were told to not make eye contact with the guards and were quickly ushered through the airport to another plane, the one that would take us to our final destination of Madras.

That plane was so small that we had to walk down the aisle hunched over and step over a hump in the middle of the floor, which I later learned was where the landing gear was! The seats were so close together that we might as well have been sitting on top of each other, not to mention that the air-conditioning was broken. I wanted off that plane ASAP! Thankfully, the flight wasn't that long, and soon enough we were on solid ground and on a bus to the mission's compound.

If you have ever seen the movie *Eat, Pray, Love*, the scenes of Julia Roberts's character traveling through the streets of India are not an exaggeration—everything was overwhelming. It was fast, furious, terrifying, loud, and there was a mix of deep ugliness and beauty. Beggars with missing limbs, oozing sores, and blind eyes crammed up against our bus to show their wounds and to try to get money. Horns were honking, cars were zipping in between each other, and I don't think any drivers used brakes; they just honked and went on.

When we finally made it to the compound, we were welcomed by leaders from the church of Palavakkam, with our missionaries interpreting their Tamil language. Our days were structured with morning devotions and then going off to the work site. We worked all day before coming back to the compound to clean up, have late-afternoon classes and Bible study, and eat supper, and then it was lights out. On the weekends we traveled to churches in the surrounding villages, and each village always had a huge celebration to honor us for our service. The people of Palavakkam were kind and welcoming. On more than one occasion, when my Sari started to unravel, someone from the congregation seated behind me would work their magic and put me back together during a hymn!

Sometimes we would go into town to shop and see the sights. I loved visiting the Hindu temples because I was amazed at the stunning architecture and craftsmanship, and the Taj Mahal was a sight to behold. I felt a deep reverence as I toured this gift of love from a husband to his wife.

Each day, we took an open-air bus to the work site. The plot of land was sandy, full of weeds, and treeless. There were several piles of bricks at the front of the property, which would be used for the footers. The church would be 30′ × 70′ and made with concrete blocks, a tin roof, and a concrete floor.

Our first order of business was to move all the bricks that were delivered to the site from the front of the plot to the back. Forming lines from the front of the property to the back, we tossed the bricks to each other. This went about as well as you could expect. Sounds of "OW!" and "HOLD UP!" rang out whenever a toss happened before the receiver was ready.

There were no facilities available to us, so we had to dig our own bathroom pit. We surrounded the hole with bricks and then fashioned a room made of branches tied together around the pit. We often had to shoo away a huge lizard that liked to hang out on the bricks surrounding the hole. I never wanted to contemplate why that lizard liked sitting there!

Drinking water also proved to be harder than I thought. We couldn't just drink any water; it had to be boiled for us. Helpers at the site would boil water for nearly 10 hours overnight, every night. It was the only way we were able to drink water without getting sick. Each morning, we filled up our water bottles with smokey-tasting warm water. It was not refreshing, yet we were very grateful that the volunteers did that for us.

After we filled our water bottles, we were handed a tool to start digging the 30′ × 70′ footers for the church. I couldn't believe that rather than a machine doing the digging, we were using our bare hands. We learned quickly that there were three ways things were done in India: the right way, the wrong way, and the India way—right or wrong. The India way was preferred by those who oversaw our building site.

Once we completed the footers, we began the brick work to build them up before starting the cinder block wall. One morning, shortly after we arrived on-site, a delivery came in the form of oxen pulling a flatbed trailer of sand, rocks, and concrete bags. Only then did we realize that we would be making our own concrete for the block work and, later, the church floor.

We had a team of four guys who mixed the concrete and dumped some into metal bowls, which were then carried to team members who laid the bricks. Much later, after the block work was completed, we had a full day of "pouring the floor." The guys mixed the concrete for the floor, this time adding in rocks, and the rest of us would lift the concrete-filled bowls, walk them to the building, and dump them to make the floor. Yes, it was a slow and tedious job. We did, however, complete the floor in one day!

The leaders of our team were very experienced and did a great job of teaching us about the different parts required to build the church. What they couldn't change, however, was the poverty that surrounded us or the tools that we used in building. Our scaffolding consisted of pieces of thin wooden branches tied together with twine, and a board was placed from end to end for us to stand on. Getting on the swaying frame was hard enough, but hauling a cinder block to complete a wall was dangerous and scary.

Being in a foreign country comes with many challenges, including language difficulties, turbulent political climates, differences in values and ways of getting a job complete ... and disease. As careful as we had all been, all of us at one time or another dealt with dysentery. We had been instructed and encouraged to never eat or drink anything in the open market that wasn't wrapped in American paper because it would have been made in India with water that had not been boiled. I tried to follow that warning but nonetheless got sick. And with my menstrual issues and how physically run down I was, when I got sick, I got really sick. My temperature was so high that I could feel the heat radiating through my jeans. Sick bay was a small building on the compound, and we would take our mats from the main room (where we slept) and lay them on the concrete floor of the sick bay until we were well enough to go back to work.

Our bathroom option at the compound was a rectangle building with three cement holes to squat over, which was an upgrade from the bathroom pit at the work site. There were doors, but the walls didn't go all the way down to the floor between stalls. Whether there were girls or boys in line, we just took whatever open spot to squat over. Modesty and dysentery do not go hand-in-hand!

I was in sick bay for at least two weeks, along with our youngest, most immature team member. They were very loud and talkative—and terrified of the scorpion that kept visiting us. At one point I yelled out, "Either kill it or let it bite me, but please stop talking about it!" I was finally told that if I didn't go back to work, I would be taken to an Indian doctor. The tone used was a cautionary one that caused me to conjure up an image that scared me, so I went back to work, still having my period and dysentery.

The job assigned to me my first day back from sick bay was laying the cinder block wall. I had to climb the scaffolding, grab a cement-filled bowl, place it onto the swaying frame underneath my feet, and grab a cinder block from a team member to lay it. Between laying a block and running to the bathroom, I was up and down multiple times. The leader finally realized that I couldn't get enough done with the way I was moving, so they sent me to measure and cut wood for another project. I still had to leave often, but at least I was on the ground and didn't have to put as much energy into going to the bathroom and getting back to work.

There were times when I didn't understand the lack of compassion from the leaders. For instance, every day I fought to stop taking the pills I knew were impacting my menstrual cycle, but they wouldn't allow me to stop taking them because they had been prescribed by a doctor.

Every night I dreamed that I was at the beginning of a long tunnel. I could see my parents and siblings at the other end, beckoning me to come home. I was so homesick that I ran through the tunnel, crying and laughing with elation that my journey was over. But when I got to the end of the tunnel, I realized that my job wasn't over and I had to go back, or I would let everyone down. I cried all the way back through the tunnel, waking up in India each morning. I began to think that I may never be able to be a missionary, wondering whether I had really been called to do this or it was just my way of trying to please God.

The days of working in 110-degree heat seemed to go on forever. What kept me going was seeing the progress being made with our building as well as meeting people from other churches in the surrounding villages. This always warmed my heart. Those experiences kept me motivated and grateful that I was doing such important work. But homesickness and my own physical health concerns kept me in a very sad state most of the time. I also felt that the call I had made was probably the wrong number, and I asked God to redial.

The missionaries on the compound were kind enough to talk with me several times and assured me that this wouldn't impede my ability to do mission work. They also reminded me that mission work is not always in a foreign country, and I could be very useful at home if working out of the country wasn't for me. This was good to hear, but it didn't align with my image of "walking the dusty roads of Damascus" and getting God's favor. The missionaries were emphatic that if God really called me to do this work, I wouldn't be able to stop thinking about or wanting it.

The India trip was a valuable life experience for me. I learned that I am stronger and more athletic than I thought I was. Although the Slough of Despond nailed me the first go-around, I successfully completed the course every day of that second week. I battled through the worst homesickness I have ever experienced and made it through the entire mission. I also learned that I can be useful and am good at laying blocks.

I will always look back on that experience with good and bad memories, but the best memory of all is the very last day on our work site. We were standing outside blessing the building in a church service for the congregation when I looked up to see the sun shining through the clouds against a deep blue sky. I knew God was pleased.

When our team finally arrived home, dressed in our saris, we were greeted by our families. My brother had made a special sign that showed me traveling to India and back, complete with the Taj Mahal and airplanes. We did a little song we made up for the group that was assembled, and then we all scattered to return to our homes.

For me, I was returning to figure out what I was called to do for the rest of my life. If field missions were not my calling, what was? And would I attend Berkshire Christian College without a major in mind?

A Moment of Grace

I do not regret being part of the mission or following a call that I believed was for me. The villagers were pleased, and I believe God was too! Job well done.

12

The Eggs Fell Out of the Basket

I was very weak when I returned home from my mission. The combination of heat, dysentery, and my menstrual cycle left me feeling done. I couldn't imagine gearing myself up to go to college in the fall, so I decided, with some nudging from my parents, to defer my entrance to college for a year.

I felt deflated. I had planned my whole life to do mission work and convinced myself that this was my calling. After I told God I felt my calling was a wrong number and asked him to "redial," I was clueless. I had absolutely no idea what my future would or should look like beyond sleeping. All my eggs had fallen out of my basket, crashed down to the ground, and were now broken. Without any options, I slipped into a depression. No one knew, though, because I still had my "Jesus facade" up, and I got busy reintegrating into home life.

Even though I just wanted to disappear, I scheduled presentations for women's groups and churches that had sponsored me for the trip. While in India, I had taken some slide photos for that purpose. The groups that had sponsored me were very attentive and asked great questions following the presentations. It lifted my spirits to show them how their money and gifts had benefited the villagers in Palavakkam, and I received so much energy from them during each presentation. Each time I returned home, however, I felt deflated again as I wrestled with what I was supposed to do with my life.

As fall approached, I became increasingly more unsettled. My parents told me I needed to focus on something and hoped I would change my mind about going to Berkshire Christian College altogether. They again pushed me to consider ASU and become a teacher; that way I could come home every weekend, and it was an in-state school with tuition that was more affordable. At the time, though, that didn't appeal to me, so I kept searching for an answer that felt right.

I took an interest inventory at the community college and, based on my answers, I was best suited for landscaping or farm management. I guess that made sense after the summer I had just spent in India. And, opposed to being in an office setting, I liked being outside—just not in 110-degree heat, jeans, or a foreign country!

Since I still didn't have a justifiable reason to go to college in Massachusetts, I decided to start at the local community college. I love animals and would never be able to send anything to slaughter, so I picked farm management over landscaping and decided on dairy farming as my focus. It seemed appropriate since my dad had worked on his father's dairy farm during his entire youth. My parents weren't sure of my choice, but they liked the fact that I wouldn't be attending Berkshire in the fall.

My first day of class was very uncomfortable. I walked into a room of guys who all stared at me. One asked, "Are you sure you're in the right room?" Clearly, they had taken time out of their farm duties to come to class.

Looking like I was starting my first day at primary school, I smiled my big smile and said, "If this is Intro to Farm Management, I am. I can tell you, though, you all know more than I will ever learn!" They laughed, and I instantly became their little sister and started getting along with them great.

I aced the paper tests, while most of the guys struggled with them. They made sure I didn't get killed or kicked by a cow at the farm, while I learned about soils and pastures and how to strip testicles and ear tag calves and cows. It was hot, difficult work, but the guys were great throughout my whole experience. I was even capable of completing the tasks, albeit awkwardly. I just had to look away when the farm dog grabbed the testicles for a snack and when the tobacco juice leaked out of the guys' mouths! I still gag thinking about that!

During that time, I still felt lost. I had stopped praying and was no longer reading my Bible. I felt very distant from God and didn't believe I had purpose; I had no idea what I was meant to do.

Though I met some great people at school, I also met some who were not so great. One guy became very controlling and scary after deciding that I needed to be his next conquest. He would lurk in dark halls and jump out at me when I was headed to class, and he would often tell me, "You will never be rid of me." I tried to tell him that I wasn't with him to begin with, but that resulted in his threatening behavior toward me. My knotted stomach and shortness of breath while walking through the halls was an indication that I feared him, yet I didn't have the skills to do anything about it. I had been raised to be nice, not complain, and not to speak my mind. I also knew that no one believed me when I did speak up. Afterall, my own parents hadn't believed that I was struck by lightning, that I lost my sense of smell following that incident, or that my going on a mission trip to India was something I was meant to do. So I never even considered speaking up to a school official.

It all came to a head one day when I was leaving school. This guy had been hiding behind another car, and as soon as I got into mine, he jumped into my passenger seat while saying, "We're going to my house."

With my heart pounding in my chest and unable to catch my breath, I whispered, "Get out."

"Drive," he said. "I'll tell you how to get there."

"I have to go home. Get out," I insisted.

"Drive, bitch, or it will hurt more when we get there."

Putting the car in drive, I tore through the parking lot as he exclaimed, "What the fuck? Slow down!"

"You either get out, or I will drive this car into oncoming traffic and kill us both!"

"You crazy bitch! Stop the car! NOW!"

I stopped the car and he stared at me.

"I don't know if you are really crazy, but all I wanted was to have a good time. I'm done with you!" Then he got out of the car and slammed the door.

Would I have driven the car into oncoming traffic? Unfortunately, at that time in my life, yes I would have. My desperation to end my suffering did not expand to thinking of another person's life or the fallout of that decision. I did feel crazy, I did feel lost, and I felt as if my life was in complete shambles.

After this incident, I would see this guy around school from time to time and was forever scared to go down the dimly lit halls that I had to travel. The fear I had developed because of his behavior lasted for years after that, and I always anticipated he would get me back for rejecting him. That was just as painful as if he had hurt me physically because the emotional scar did not heal well.

Around this time, I remembered a coach at Berkshire who was always at our church camps and did outreach for admissions. I called him one day and talked with him about why I didn't come to Berkshire and what I was doing.

"It sounds like it isn't working out the way you planned," he said. "Have you ever thought of doing youth ministry? Coming to Berkshire without a plan won't hurt you; you'll find your way. You can still come. I can tell the registrar you'll be coming in the fall. It doesn't matter that you'll start later in the year. God's timing is never our timing."

My heart rate lowered, my eyes welled up with tears, and I wanted to just let go. It was such a relief to hear him say, "You can still come." Perhaps God was still calling me and I would still be okay.

"I'll do it," I said. "Expect to see me in the fall."

"That's great, Midge. I'll let the registrar know. You'll be hearing from her."

And with that, a glimmer of hope returned.

A Moment of Grace

I never learned how to appropriately speak up for myself, and for that I give myself grace. I could have put many people's lives in peril, and I am grateful that my recklessness didn't hurt anyone.

13

Berkshire Christian College

In the fall of 1979, I was packed and ready to begin my journey to Berkshire Christian College, located in the quaint and beautiful town of Lenox, Massachusetts. The college was set high up on a hill overlooking a valley, and the fall leaves were exploding in glorious colors. Music from the Tanglewood Symphony could be heard as students sat on the hill and took a break from their classes.

At least, that is the vision I had of where I was headed, but I still had to get out of my hometown. There were five of us from North Carolina heading to Berkshire that fall, and we were scheduled to meet up and then load into a van that would take us all up together.

My parents took me to the pickup spot, where I said my goodbyes to Momma and Ethan (my sister was already married and living in Raleigh). I loaded my things and got into the van, with $45 in my pocket.

Daddy came up to the van and said to me, "If you go through with this, I will not send you a dime of my money."

I looked back at him to see his face stern with angry eyes. My heart broke as I said, "Don't send a penny; I will send it back."

With that, Daddy stepped away from the van, the door closed, and we headed out of the parking lot. My eyes burned with tears that I refused to let fall. I quickly swallowed all the emotions and started planning how I was really going to make this work. My stomach was lurching, and I was really scared that I wouldn't be able to do it, yet I knew I had no other options at that point. Once again, without any real meaningful conversation with God, I had put all my eggs into one basket. It had to work out. I wasn't planning to ever come home again.

After a 14-hour drive, we finally arrived on campus. The campus was small, with a student body consisting of 140 students, 40 of whom lived off campus. Vannah Hall was the only large building. It was set high up on the hill and held all our classrooms (except for music classes, which were held in the chapel) and the bookstore, where we signed up for classes. The chapel, music rooms, kitchen, and a lounge area that had games and a TV were in a red barn-like building down the driveway from the classrooms. At the bottom of the hill, to the right of the walkway, was the boys' dormitory, and continuing down the walkway to the left was the girls' dormitory. The hill was affectionately known as "Hernia Hill" because it was a long haul back up from the dorms in blizzard conditions, especially when we were carrying books while hurrying to class. We often had to hold onto the rail during high winds to avoid being pushed over.

Once I was assigned to my dorm room, I realized that I would be rooming with one of my friends from our church conference. I was happy about that, and I was really excited about just being there! We started to unpack our things when I heard a Southern drawl outside our window. I stuck my head out and said, "Who is that Southern voice?"

A bright-blond-haired guy looked up and said, "I'm Sam from Georgia."

"Well, hi Georgia! I'm Midge from North Carolina!"

He paused as the rest of his friends went on ahead of him. "We're heading to the swimming pool, do you wanna come?"

"Sure! I'll be right down!"

My roommate said to me, "We haven't finished unpacking yet."

I was stunned. Pausing for a moment to collect my thoughts, I said, "Well, I know I haven't unpacked yet, but I know what I didn't pack, and that is my momma. I'll get it done when I get back. Do you want to come?"

She declined.

With that, I changed into my bathing suit and headed out the door. To say the least, we didn't stay roommates for long. I made sure I paid for my own space every year so I could have a private room.

That Monday morning, I went to the registrar's office to discuss money. My conversation with her was short and sweet. With only one small, basic grant and now less than $45 in my pocket after buying snacks on the trip, I would have to take out massive student loans and get a job, possibly two.

After I talked with a girl in my dorm about my financial concerns, she offered to introduce me to Mom Flynn, who ran the kitchen and hired students to work as servers. I interviewed with her and was hired!

I worked in the kitchen the entire four years I was at Berkshire. Mom Flynn always meant the world to me, and her guidance and toughness took me out of my head many times. One convocation day, I forgot to bring my work shoes and all I had were my high heels. When I explained to Mom Flynn what had happened, she said, "You don't have time to go get anything else, so you are going to have to make do."

When I put on my uniform, I looked down and realized that with my high heels, my pants were way too short. I thought perhaps I could stay on the sidelines and fill bowls instead of walking on the floor. No such luck. Mom Flynn instructed me to go see about a table in the back, and after I turned to ask another server to go, she belted, "Did I call you by the wrong name? Get out there now!"

I walked as fast as I could out to the far back left table, where a group of my friends sat. After getting their order, I started back to the front. Everything was quiet in the dining hall, and I was racing back to the front before anyone saw me with my high water pants I heard, "Noah, Noah Noble, are you expecting a flood?"

I froze, everyone started giggling, and with a red face I practically sprinted back to the front and asked for what I needed. Mom Flynn handed me the bowl and I paused. She said, "Well, are you going to take that before it gets cold?"

"Yes, ma'am." I walked back through the snickers and toward my friends.

"Very funny!" I laughed.

"We're only picking; we couldn't pass that up."

For the rest of my time at Berkshire, whenever I committed a foul in basketball, my friend who was a game announcer would say, "And that foul was committed by Noah Noble!" Although it was embarrassing, it was also fun to have a nickname. That year, when Halloween rolled around, I dressed up in a bright-yellow raincoat, put stuffed animals in my pockets, and went as Noah.

My first year was going well. I had the kitchen work, I found another job cleaning a lady's very large house, and I was hired to pour champagne at one of their Christmas gatherings. Money was tight, but with my student loans I was making it. I joined the soccer team as a way of working out. I had no intention of playing, but after the goalie graduated I became first string. That is how small Berkshire was! I had never seen or played soccer; I just wanted to lose weight! Everyone tried out for goalie but, when all was said and done, I was selected. I held that position for all four years, ending my career with several shutouts.

Though I had a dream of majoring in Christian ministry, that plan got derailed early on in my first year. The president of the college called me into his office to talk about my major, explaining that "Our denomination does not pay anyone to do youth ministries. You can major in that as well as earn your BA in theology, with the required Bible classes in addition to your other major. The problem is you will not graduate with a degree that will get you hired. Unless you're planning to get married before you leave school, I suggest you take advantage of my wife's new teaching curriculum that she's starting this year."

I was floored. I don't know what upset me the most—his belief that I needed to get married or that my second plan to be worthy in God's sight was now being taken away? I thought about whether I would find a husband in the next four years, and the thought of that made me sick to my stomach. I didn't know why.

Stammering, I said, "I just started dating my boyfriend. I don't know if I'll be married, but I really want to major in youth ministry."

"That's fine. You can have a double major in that and education so you can work as a teacher and get paid and can volunteer at the church of your choice in the youth department. Here's the brochure. Classes start next week, so you better get signed up today."

"Um, thank you," I said as I took the brochure and then left his office.

As I walked down to the registrar to register for my new classes and pay for the required books, I thought, *A teacher, just like Daddy.* I had wanted to be that when I was younger; to be liked by my dad. Then I wanted to be a missionary to be liked by God. Even though this should have been a teachable moment, I was still living in fear and denial. It wasn't time to put the pieces together.

When Christmas vacation came during my freshman year, the sting of the last words I shared with my dad were still burning hot in my mind and heart. I turned down all the rides offered to me, and I was left with no ride home. *Perfect!*

When Momma called to check what time I would be home for Christmas, I told her, "Momma, all the cars are full. I don't have a ride."

"How can they all be full?" she asked. "You all went together to get there."

"That was a van, and we were all going to the same place. Now we're all going to different locations."

"Well, you have to come home for Christmas."

"I'm sorry, Momma."

After hanging up the phone, I talked it over with my boyfriend Henry. "I'm going to fly home," he said.

"I don't have the money for that," I responded.

"What are you going to do?"

"I'll stay here and catch up on reading, walk in the snow, and sleep!"

The next call I got from home was from my dad. "Your mom tells me that you don't have a ride home for Christmas. You will break your Momma's heart if you don't come home."

"Well, Daddy, I can't help it. The cars are full."

"I will send you a plane ticket. You are coming home for Christmas."

"Daddy, you can't afford that," I replied, trying to conceal my anger at him throwing out money to me after our last conversation. I didn't see this as an olive branch; it felt controlling.

"It will have to be a round-trip ticket Daddy; I have to get back for the next term."

"I know that. How dumb do you think I am? I will send the ticket. Just get yourself home."

We said our goodbyes.

A week before Christmas, I received an envelope in the mail. My plane ticket was inside. One ticket. I called home.

"Daddy, I got the ticket, but it's only one way. I have to have a round-trip ticket so I can get back to school."

"You don't need them both right now. Your return ticket is here."

"Really?" I asked.

"Are you calling me a liar?"

"No, Daddy, I just thought you would send them both."

The conversation ended with me still feeling manipulated, without really having any evidence that I was.

As it happened, Henry and I took the same flight. We weren't sitting together, but it was nice to have him at the airport with me.

When I arrived at the airport in North Carolina, my family and I exchanged all the standard pleasantries. I felt awkward hugging my dad, and the hug I received from him was aloof, not a genuine connection as expected. My younger brother was excited to see me, as was my mom.

When I got home and went into my bedroom, I looked for the return trip ticket on my dresser. It wasn't there. Feeling fear in the pit of my stomach, I finished unpacking while my mind swirled with questions, catastrophic outcomes, and plans to get back to Berkshire without a car. I went out into the living room and asked my dad, "Where is the return ticket? I didn't see it on my dresser."

Without looking up from his paper, he said, "I didn't get a round-trip ticket. You don't need to go back to Berkshire. You can get an education degree at Appalachian State. It's cheaper."

"You promised!" I exclaimed.

"This makes more sense."

I bolted out of the room and into my bedroom, slamming the door. Thankfully, in that moment, neither parent chose to come down and yell at me for that.

My thoughts were racing, and I felt panicked and trapped. *How will I get back? It takes 14 hours to drive it! I don't have the money to buy a ticket. How would I get somewhere to buy it? They wouldn't let me use the car; they might think I'd drive it to Berkshire! I don't even know how to go! I was drugged out on Dramamine the whole trip up! OMG, they won't ever let me leave.* Then it came to me. I could hitchhike back. *That's it!* I thought, *I have a way out.*

All freshman year, without a car of my own, I had been hitchhiking to many places. Everyone was worried about it, and no one at school wanted me to do it. There were several incidents when I could have been in real trouble. Thankfully, my guardian angels (yes,

I required more than one) worked overtime that year on my behalf. I was reckless, brazen, and didn't care about my own safety or health. One of my rides was in the back of a van, loaded with guys who were drinking. Telling me to sit on a bucket between the seats near the front, the driver said, "You remind me of my little sister. If it weren't for that, I'd let them have their way with you. This was dangerous; don't do it again." And that wasn't the only unsafe decision I made while hitchhiking; I took other rides with drunk drivers and surly characters. I was on the edge and didn't realize how much I didn't care if I fell off. So I knew that I would be on the road again, thumbing it back to school.

With this realization, I went into the kitchen to use the wall phone and dialed Ruth, one of my friends at school. Whispering into the phone, I said, "Daddy didn't buy a round-trip ticket. I don't have a way to get back to school unless I hitchhike, so just tell the registrar I will start back after Christmas Day, and I will get there as soon as I can."

"Don't you dare do that," Ruth said.

"I have to, Ruth. I am not staying here."

"Just give me a minute. I will think of something, but don't leave your house until you hear from me. Promise me!"

"I promise I won't leave until the day after Christmas, so you have a couple of days to come up with a plan because I only have one that I know of."

"If I sent you a ticket, would they take you to the airport?"

"I wouldn't count on it."

"Right. Okay, I'll call you back, so just stay put."

The very next day, I got a call from Ruth. "Here's the plan. Louise and I are going to come pick you up the day or two after Christmas."

"What? You can't do that! It is a 14-hour trip!"

"I know that, but we are coming, and you had better be there when we get there. Give me your address and answer this question: Will your parents shoot me when I pull up in the driveway?"

Laughing, I said, "Absolutely not. You'll think I'm lying. They'll greet you with smiles, thank you for what you're doing for me, and welcome you into our home like you're family."

"Well, that's better than being shot. I believe you, you know. I don't care how they act toward me and Louise; I believe you."

"Thank you," I said through my tears. "I really appreciate this."

I boldly left that phone call with hope in my heart, then walked into the living room and told my parents that my friends were coming to get me after Christmas.

"What?" asked Momma. "They're coming here? Where will they sleep? What are they going to eat?"

"They'll eat what I eat and there's room in the bedroom for all of us."

"You have twin beds."

"We have the pullout couch downstairs."

"Why are they coming?" Daddy asked.

"Because I didn't have a way back to school."

"So, what, you told them I'm a liar?" Daddy said as he glared at me.

I looked away and replied, "I didn't call you a liar. I just told them there wasn't a ticket here to return to school."

Daddy went back to watching TV and didn't talk about it again.

Early in the morning, two days after Christmas, the girls arrived. My parents greeted them exactly as I had predicted.

I closed the door to the bedroom, and we all started giggling.

"My God," Ruth said, "I feel like we're in the Twilight Zone."

"They don't own guns, do they?" asked Louise.

Laughing, I said, "Daddy does, but he doesn't keep it loaded. By the time he remembers where the bullets are, we can be gone! Don't worry; they'll keep up with this charade until we leave." The girls planned to leave the next day so that we could be back at school on time.

I could tell by the way my parents were acting that they weren't pleased, but they kept up the show for the rest of the day and were gushing with gratitude the next morning when we left. I knew then that that would be the last time I would fall for something like this.

For the rest of my college experience, I spent time with friends during the short Thanksgiving breaks, spent Christmas breaks taking winter classes, worked camps in the summer, and only saw my parents when they showed up for our choir performances when we sang near our hometown. I was never sent a care package. They never saw me play volleyball, soccer, or basketball. They never came to visit. Momma was faithful about calling, and I would call her from time to time, but my parents never acknowledged the depth of my college experience.

I built a very strong wall around my heart during those four years in college. I allowed myself to believe that my parents didn't really love me, which made my decisions easier because the guilt of hurting their feelings would have devastated me. I was living the life I had wanted to live, attending Berkshire, singing in the Chorale, and learning about the Bible and how to defend my faith. I was about to discover, however, that my experience at Berkshire was going to go sideways.

A Moment of Grace

My parents lived on very little money and were always worried that we wouldn't make it. I believe they tried to protect me from incurring debt. Though that doesn't take the hurt of betrayal away, it allows me to give them grace.

Major Crush

It was my second year at Berkshire, and I was chilling in the dorm with Ruth, watching all the new students arrive looking confused and overwhelmed. I felt grateful that I didn't have to do that this year!

As Ruth and I talked, I noticed someone approaching the dorms. They had thin, short hair and walked with a wide stance. Wearing blue jeans, they had a huge silver key ring attached to their belt, a ring so full of keys that it swung and clinked with every step. Upon entering the dorm, they walked past us at a very quick clip, threw up a right hand, uttered a deep "hey," and kept on going.

I looked at Ruth, and she looked back at me with a shocked expression.

"That was a guy, right?" I asked.

"I don't know," she said. "Maybe it was maintenance."

"Shouldn't he have announced himself?"

Later, I was introduced to this person, whose name was Kay, and she was not a guy. Kay was a freshman and had come to Berkshire with her high school sweetheart, who was also a freshman. As we began talking and hanging out together, I felt an immediate kinship with her. She had a good sense of humor, and our connection became very strong, very quickly.

As our friendship deepened, Kay and I began calling each other "IFs" (inseparable friends). We did everything together and, having decided on not going back to Hickory, I would go to her home on short breaks. I wasn't jealous of her boyfriend, but I realized that I had deep feelings for her. They were not sexual feelings, but I felt a deep emotional connection and missed her terribly when she went home for visits or out on dates with her boyfriend.

I also realized that we were on two different levels when it came to motivation. I didn't notice this at the time, but as I look back on our time together and some conversations we had later, it has become more apparent that she was probably dealing with depression.

To attend Berkshire, Kay had to get a job, and she was hired in maintenance. One of her jobs was to chop wood that was used for the classroom fireplaces. Vannah Hall was an old two-story building with high ceilings and large rooms, so its fireplaces were crucial in keeping us warm and, most probably, in cutting down on the electricity bill. Kay wasn't always able to get up in the morning to see to her responsibilities. It wasn't because she was a slacker; she had worked in a factory at home and was very productive and worked hard, long hours in horrible heat. Yet with the demands of college and the inclement weather that made us all want to stay snug in our blankets in the morning, Kay found it almost impossible to get up.

Taking on the role of caretaker, I tried to make sure she got up, sometimes literally pulling her out of bed! This was not very effective, and our relationship became very unhealthy. I became the mother and enforcer and would get quite angry when she didn't get up. I tried to reason with her and convince her that she would have to leave school if she couldn't keep a job, but toward the end, she didn't seem to care.

She literally quit going to classes and showing up for work, and the day came when she had to withdraw from college.

With the news that she would be leaving, we both cried the loudest, longest, and most gut-wrenching cry I have ever experienced. I felt as if my world had ended. We prayed and we cried some more. Miraculously, someone donated money to help Kay stay in school. She was going to have to change her ways, and I desperately hoped that she could do it.

Our relationship continued to deepen, and I had no doubt that, somehow, we would always be together. What I didn't know was why my connection with her was so deep. I had no clue that I was experiencing a massive crush. The longer we were together, the deeper my feelings grew. I just never realized that I loved her in a way that I couldn't admit to. Though I didn't realize it at the time, these were similar to feelings I had had for a friend in junior high, though not on such a deep level; in hindsight, that had been my first real crush. Even though I dated Henry and loved him, my feelings for Kay were different. Only in retrospect can I admit that I found her physically attractive.

I dearly cared about Henry, but I wasn't sure what that meant. One day, we went to his mother's home and walked her property. Taking me to a section of the property, he showed me where we would build our home after we were married. I immediately felt sick to my stomach. Smiling at Henry, I told him the property was beautiful, but all the while I could feel the panic swelling up inside of me, reminiscent of dating someone who wanted to get intimate. I left that visit with lots of concerns about my future with Henry, but I also desperately wanted him to stay in my life. I figured that I had plenty of time before we would be married, and neither of us wanted to do anything before we graduated.

Our relationship took a rapid turn the next year. Partway through the year, Henry called and told me he thought things wouldn't work out between the two of us.

"What do you mean? What's wrong?" I asked.

"It's not that anything is wrong. I really like you. But I just don't think we need to get married."

"I don't need to get married right now either," I said, "We don't have to break up!"

"I just don't think you're the right person for me to marry."

My heart dropped, and I felt panicked. All I could utter was, "Okay."

"I still want to be your friend," Henry said.

"Okay," I whispered, and then hung up.

I was devastated. Not because we weren't going to be married, but because the feeling of not being good enough swelled up inside of me.

The next day confirmed my belief of unworthiness when I saw Henry walking hand-in-hand with a freshman who was pretty and thin. I was embarrassed and saw the eyes of my classmates looking at me as the new couple walked past us.

A subtle shift happened during this time, manifesting in a physical complication that met my emotional needs. I got the flu and was nauseous all the time, but I had trouble throwing up. One of the girls told me that I could make myself throw up and I would feel so much better.

"Yuck!" I said. "I don't think I could do that."

"Sure you can. I do it all the time. There's nothing wrong with it and you'll feel better. Just stick your finger to the back of your throat, and your body will do the rest."

"That's gross."

"Well, you can feel better or stay sick," she said, walking off.

I went into the bathroom, and after a few failed attempts, I threw up. Remarkably, I felt lighter and the pit in my stomach felt better. This began my subtle skill of purging.

I convinced myself that I was doing it because of the flu and so that I could feel less nauseous in class and on the soccer field. It became an insidious way of dealing with my anxiety, my broken heart, and my dislike of myself. Anytime I was upset, I would make time to purge. Years and years of swallowing the opinions of others, enduring emotional pain that couldn't be spoken, and suffering through my own internal struggles were managed and lightened momentarily by purging.

At first I only vomited once a day, but that soon escalated as each purge gave me a euphoric emotional release. I began purging after every meal. My stomach could no longer handle being full, and intaking any food soon became uncomfortable. In the back of my mind, I was still fixated on the thin girl Henry preferred. I knew in my heart that I wasn't good enough. Without allowing myself to realize it, I began vomiting whenever I was angry, sad, scared, or anxious. I stopped eating when I could get away with it, and if challenged, I would eat and then take care of it soon afterward. I felt empowered by this. Never again could someone make me do anything without my taking charge later.

I didn't realize how insane this was and that my coping skill was not coping at all. I was far from having any true, authentic power, but since I was losing weight I was feeling a heightened sense of euphoria because I was finally the thin one. From my sophomore year through my senior year, I was cycling between bulimia and anorexia, binging and starving so I could deal with life.

Kay figured out what I was doing, and we had many fights about it, but we stayed friends all through college. She even decided to come home with me to North Carolina for a week after I graduated.

My senior year came quicker than I would have liked. Berkshire was my Utopia and I loved New England. Knowing that I would be heading back south after graduation increased my anxiety. Once again, I was summoned into the president's office. I had done what he had suggested and was graduating with a BA in theology and a K-12 teaching certificate. I saw him glance up from his desk as I walked in, and then he looked out the window. I sat down and he turned his gaze back on me.

"So," he said, "you'll be graduating this year."

"Yes, sir, that is the plan."

"Well, for that to be a reality, we need to talk about something quite serious."

My heart skipped a beat and I felt my face flush.

"It has come to my attention," he continued, "that you have lost a lot of weight. I think you may be suffering from an eating disorder."

"I eat!" I exclaimed. "I'm fine."

"Well, I don't want to imply that you're lying, but my wife will not recommend you for graduation if you can't be a good role model for the students you serve."

"She can't stop me if I've completed all my course credits."

"Yes, she can. If she feels one of her students is unfit, she can expect that student to complete therapy or any other medical intervention before she signs off on graduation requirements."

I was stunned. My thoughts raced through my mind as I searched for a defense, and I couldn't pull one together.

The president continued, "I'm going to be watching you carefully, and I suggest that you come to me for counseling. Let's see how that goes, and then I'll expect a session with you and your parents before you leave for home."

"So, you and I will talk a few times and that will be enough for me to graduate?"

"That will be a beginning, and I will expect that other people who love you will be able to confirm that you're eating, and my wife will also be a part of the final decision. Do you have any questions?"

I wanted to sprint out of that office and slam the door behind me. Instead I replied, "No sir, thank you."

"I can see you tomorrow afternoon once your classes are over and before you go into work."

"Yes sir," I said, walking to the door feeling faint and terrified. I didn't know what was worse—going through four years of college and not graduating or having the president of the college talk to my parents.

As I made my way back to the dorm, I was fueled with anger and fear. All I could think about doing was eating something and purging it … and that is exactly what I did. Then I did what I had always done: I became the model student and client, got even more secretive, and when it was time for the family session, I was all smiles and exceptionally positive. My parents were stunned by my appearance and, when they participated in the family session, my dad was quick to say, "This stops now. We will take it from here."

With that behind me, I was able to graduate and go back to North Carolina with Kay. We had a great week, but my life with her would not be what I had imagined. Her inability to manage my eating disorder created a distance that our friendship wouldn't survive.

A Moment of Grace

I know that I needed an intervention. Though I will never agree with how the school president used his power to change my choices, and though I wasn't able to stop him, I appreciate that someone cared enough to step in and try to get me healthy.

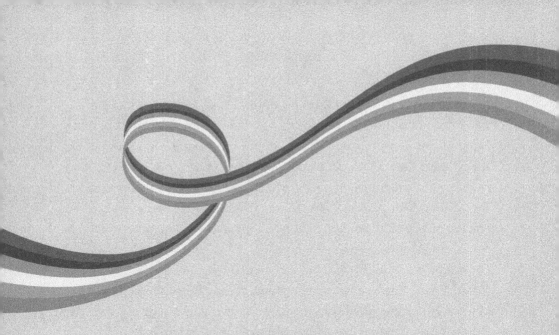

As long as I am still above ground and still breathing, I am not done.

—MIDGE NOBLE

Wild-Haired Boy

I left Massachusetts and returned to North Carolina in the summer of 1982 and began working four jobs. I was a substitute teacher for three surrounding counties, a private tutor, a choir director for my grandfather's church, and a Pizza Hut waitress. After working for a few months as a second-grade substitute teacher, I realized that teaching school would not allow me to help kids on the level I wanted to help them. I knew this the minute I sat in the hall listening to the story of a wild-haired boy who ran everywhere he went.

    This boy tugged at my heart from the moment I met him. He was unkempt, his hair looked as if it had never seen a brush, his clothes were not always clean, and neither was he; he looked neglected to me. He was bursting with energy all day long and he never slowed down. I had to tell him to walk, ask him to put his eyes on me so he could hear directions, and redirect him constantly so he could get his morning work done. I was not sure whether he was getting the loving attention he needed at home, and I felt drawn to him in a very protective way.

One morning, as I stood in the hall to monitor the car line entries and welcome my students into the classroom, I saw my little wild-haired boy come into the building. He *walked* into the school after getting out of the car, *walked* down the hall and into our classroom, sat down, and put his head on his desk. I knew something was wrong. At that moment, I didn't care about the reading groups or the multiplication tables; I cared about him. I wanted to sit with him in whatever pain he was in and let his story come out.

After I requested my teaching assistant start the reading groups and instructed the other students to begin their morning work, I asked my wild-haired boy, whose head was still down on his desk, to come out into the hall with me. As I sat down on the floor next to him, his head hung down.

"What's wrong?" I asked.

Without looking up, he said, "I hit my head on the car when I got out."

Looking at his head, I noticed he did have a bump. Knowing that his dad always dropped him off, I replied, "Ouch! Did you tell your dad?"

"No," he said, "he already knew it was hurt."

"Did he?"

"Yeah," he said, "because the knife hit it last night."

"What?" I exclaimed, probably a little too enthusiastically.

He looked up for the first time and then back down again.

"How did a knife hit your head?" I asked as gently as I could.

He paused for a moment, and I was afraid he would clam up, but he continued: "You know that game your dad plays with you?"

"Which one?"

"The one where you stand with your legs apart and your daddy throws the knife in between them?" He looked up to see my response.

"Oh, that game," I said with a solemn face. "Did the blade hit your head?"

"No, silly, the handle," he replied with a smile. "The blade would have cut me. I was lucky."

"Yes, yes you were," I said. "I am glad you're okay. Take it easy this morning and just rest. I can go over your multiplication tables with you later."

Of course, I had to inform the principal, who then informed the school counselor. The moment I had to hand his story over to them was the moment my career path changed. Right then, I wanted to find out how to be the person, the therapist, the counselor, or whoever it was who could help him more.

My little wild-haired boy never came back to my classroom before the end of the school year. When I asked the principal a week after this event whether he knew what had happened with the report, he told me that I was not credentialed to have that information. All he said was, "I wouldn't expect him back."

That really bothered me. My heart hurt for all the boy had been through and may still be going through. I could only hope that he was getting the help he needed and that, while he was in my classroom, he felt heard and knew he mattered.

Graduate school became my focus after that experience. I later chose to do the school counseling track since I already had a teaching certificate and experience working in a school setting. I deferred my college loans, made plans to add graduate school to that loan, paid off my car, got permission to stay with my aunt and uncle who lived in Boone, North Carolina, and applied to the Counselor Education and Research Graduate Program at ASU, affectionately known as App State. Unfortunately, I missed the cutoff date for the Graduate Records Exam, but the registrar assured me that I could come into the program in August on a provisional basis and then take the test in October.

I also applied for and was accepted to work as a graduate assistant in the Counselor Education and Research Department. I started work immediately, answering phones, taking messages, and reading some of the literature in the study room that was off the lobby. It was nice to have time to acclimate before the professors had work for us. And there, in that tiny little office, is where I would meet the love of my life.

> ### A Moment of Grace
>
> I don't know what demons my wild-haired boy's father had. I hope he was able to work through them. Though I understand that we are all human, I find it hard to imagine putting your own child in danger. I will never know whether the family was able to be reunited, and I hope that my wild-haired boy grew up to have a wonderful life. Being unable to help this child directly was a defining moment in my life that changed my trajectory from teaching to counseling.

16

The Love Story Begins

I was reading in the study room at the counselor education office when I stood up and noticed a girl sitting on the couch out in the lobby. She had on blue jeans and a maroon sweatshirt with gray sleeves. Her hair was short, and she was wearing one sneaker. Her right foot and ankle were in a cast, and crutches were leaning against the couch.

I walked out and said, "Hi, I'm Midge."

"I'm Mary."

As a side note, she will tell you now that she had definitely checked me out while I was reading; she remembers me wearing bright-yellow shorts, sandals, and a multicolored short sleeved shirt.

"Do you need any help?" I asked, assuming she was a student who needed to see an advisor.

"No, I actually work here."

"Oh, cool, so do I! I'm on the school counseling track."

"I'm focusing on mental health counseling."

"We may be in some classes together."

"We probably will."

"What happened to your ankle?"

"I had to have surgery because of a softball injury."

"Ouch!"

"It's okay. I should be out of the cast soon."

"I was just headed out to register for classes. I'm sure it'll be a little busier than where I went."

"Where was that?"

"Berkshire Christian College in Lenox, Massachusetts. We only had about 140 students."

"Wow! I was an undergrad here, so I'm familiar with the setup. I'd be glad to go with you and help you out."

"Oh no, that's not necessary. With your foot? You need to stay put!"

"I get myself around campus all the time. I'm happy to help."

"Thank you, but I'll be fine. I'll probably see you later."

"Okay, good luck."

I could have stayed there and talked to Mary forever. I really loved the idea of her walking with me to the gym so we could talk some more. I experienced an instant connection with her, which kind of rattled me. However, after everything that I had been through with Kay, I was not ready to get too close to anyone.

I walked down toward the gym, thinking the whole time about how much I wished that I were still talking to Mary and getting to know her better. When I reached the gym, I followed a crowd down the steps to the very lowest section. The door opened to a massive floor with tables and people everywhere! I had absolutely no idea what to do or where to start. I got into the wrong line and was told I needed a photo ID to register for any classes. As I was trying to find out where to go for that, I saw Mary coming toward me on her crutches.

"Hey!" she said, "How's it going?"

"It's a lot different."

"What have you signed up for?"

THE LOVE STORY BEGINS

"Nothing! I have to get registered and get a photo ID first."
"Do you know where it is?"
"Not yet."
"Come on. I did it yesterday, so I can show you."

I felt immediate relief and instinctively knew that I was in good hands.

The next day, I again saw Mary at the counselor education office. She told me about her dog, Sheba, a small shepherd mix she had rescued one winter on a walk down a snow-covered road in Boone, North Carolina. I talked about always wanting a Labrador retriever but never being able to get one. Mary told me about her roommate's dog, Jo Jo, who tore up everything!

Spending time with Mary was so easy. It was like we had known each other before and were falling back into conversation as if we had never been separated. Mary also had the gift of really seeing me—more than I ever saw myself. She could also see that my bravado was a mask for anxiety and uncertainty, and she was very diligent at holding me accountable for the answers I gave her. If she got a hint that I was using the FINE word (feelings inside not expressed) she would patiently encourage me to find a specific feeling. The more we talked, the deeper our connection became. We were virtually inseparable except for when we went to our respective houses to sleep.

The day I met Mary's roommate validated what I had guessed. She walked into the office where I was working and stood in front of the desk.

"May I help you?" I asked.
"I'm looking for Mary."
"Mary Anderson?"
"Are you Midge?"
"Yes. How do you know that?"
"I am Mary's roommate, Shelby."

"Oh!" I said, and then took a closer look. Shelby had short, dark-black hair in a bobbed cut. She was wearing a red flannel shirt, wide belt, and jeans, was short, and had a great smile.

"I haven't seen Mary lately. I'm not sure when she'll be back."

Smiling that big smile again, she said, "No problem. She's probably at home, so I'll catch up with her there. You should come to supper one night."

"Oh," I said, "that would be nice." And off she went.

I thought to myself, *She must be gay*. I had read that gay women wear flannel and wide belts (yes, I know how this sounds), and I had thought Mary might be gay when I first met her, but I kept putting it out of my mind. I didn't want to get in the middle of Mary and her roommate, so at this point I wasn't sure if I should go to dinner with them if they invited me. As if this weren't enough pressure, I hadn't told Mary that I was bulimarexic. It was easier to meet for coffee or go for hikes instead of real meals.

The next day, Mary came into the study room and asked me to come to dinner. I started to make an excuse, but then she said, "It will just be you and me, my roommate is going out of town."

"Oh, well, if she wouldn't mind," I stammered, "that would be great." I wasn't at the point where I could just say no.

"How about tonight?" she asked.

"Sure, let me call my uncle and just let him know."

"Okay, I'll wait in the office."

This began the *longest* drive I have ever had in my life! We headed out of Boone and drove for what seemed like forever, making twists and turns and going higher and higher up the mountain. I was having a conversation with Mary, while my brain was in overdrive.

What if she really is gay? Is she going to want to have sex with me? Where is she taking me? Are we still in North Carolina? I could never find my way back to campus! OMG, this is what the youth leader warned us

THE LOVE STORY BEGINS

about: *"Homosexuals will get you alone and the only thing they think about is having sex."* Then I would try to reel my brain back in and remind myself, *Mary is really nice, and she's a very caring and thoughtful person. She would never mistreat me. I really like her and enjoy her company, but where in the hell are we going?*

Finally, we made it up this very long, steep, gravel road to a little wooden house with a basement apartment below. There wasn't another soul anywhere around! I heard a dog bark and Mary remarked, "That's Sheba. She has some trouble trusting people."

Mary went into the apartment first and greeted Sheba, who came up and sat in front of me as I came inside. Wanting to make a good impression, I immediately bent over to say hello to Sheba, and in return, she growled and snapped at me—almost biting my nose!

"Wow!" I exclaimed.

"SHEBA!" Mary called and gave her the "No" correction and then addressed me. "Like I said, she's been abused and isn't quick to trust anyone. Are you okay?"

"Got it!" I said. "My fault."

The apartment was very small. The kitchen, dinette table, and living area were in one long rectangular room, a bathroom was right past the dinette table, and a bedroom was off the room next to a daybed. Cozy! The apartment also had a free-standing wood stove next to the daybed on one side of the wall and a coffee table, TV, and another chair across the room.

Mary started up the grill. She had chosen steaks to grill with some vegetables, and she offered me a beer, which I gladly took. Our conversation flowed with ease, and I was having the best time. Even Sheba seemed to warm up to me.

Following dinner, I excused myself to the bathroom. As you recall, it was right off the main room. Have you ever thrown up quietly? I had a technique that I thought was great, but I learned later, not all the time!

When I came out, Mary never said a word and I figured I had pulled it off.

"Dinner was really great. Thanks for having me," I said. "I guess I need to get back though."

"You're welcome. I hope you'll come again. I know Shelby was wanting you to come."

"Yeah, sure, I would love to."

Mary drove me back down that long road to my car in the campus parking lot. This would be the first of many evenings I spent with Mary. I planned to bring my car from then on so that Mary wouldn't have to drive me back. As it turned out, there would be a day that I didn't need to drive back after dinner.

When I returned home, my uncle was still awake. After he came in to say good night and I hugged him, he took a step back and said, "Are you doing drugs?"

"NO!" I exclaimed.

"I smell it on you!"

"I had a beer at supper. I'm not doing drugs."

"Well, I can't have that stuff in my house!"

"Of course not, I would never."

He said good night and went back to his room.

I was stunned and felt embarrassed that he would believe I would do drugs. It took me a long time to get to sleep after that.

The next day, Mary told me that Shelby was disappointed that I had been to dinner without her there and wanted Mary to invite me back up that weekend.

It was odd going back to Mary's apartment with Shelby there. They seemed like best friends, but then there were times that Shelby would put her arm around Mary, and once I saw Mary put her arm behind Shelby's back and rest her hand in the back pocket of Shelby's jeans. Shelby told stories about their life together and Mary stayed quiet.

THE LOVE STORY BEGINS

At one point, Shelby turned to me and said, "So, you want to date my girlfriend?"

"NO!" I exclaimed, "I'm not gay! Really, I don't want to get in the middle of anything!"

Mary glared at Shelby and said, "That's enough."

It makes me laugh now. Who was I trying to convince? Shelby just grinned that big grin and sarcastically said, "Right, you're not gay! Glad I don't have anything to worry about."

Shortly after that night, it became clear that Mary and Shelby were having problems. Mary didn't share much, but Shelby was gone on the weekends when I went to dinner at Mary's house.

Mary and I had so much in common. We loved sports, hiking, hanging out, listening to music, and reading and would spend our entire weekends together. After having a beer with dinner, I slept on the daybed rather than going back to my uncle's house.

Here is where things start to get a little crazy. Although I had no idea that I was gay, my feelings for Mary were getting stronger. Mary's feelings for me were deep, and it was difficult for her to keep them in check. As we would drive places together, she would reach over and hold my hand and tell me how glad she was that I was in her life. I would leave her notes on her car before leaving campus at night, thinking that I was just being a very thoughtful friend. We were always hugging or holding hands, but I thought it was just friendly. I had seen boys and girls in India hanging on each other while walking down the street and being very affectionate toward each other. They didn't seem to have the same hang-ups about touching that we do in the United States. But I was still uncomfortable and said one time, "You know, if people see us holding hands in the car, they may get the wrong idea."

Mary would just smile, squeeze my hand, and say, "Why can't friends hold hands?"

Then there was the time that Mary came over to my uncle's house and we were sitting on the couch close together and had been holding hands. The electricity between us was palpable. My uncle came in unexpectedly and said, "Hey, what are you two doing?"

We moved apart and I said something lame, like, "Nothing, we're just talking."

After looking at me for a long time, my uncle said, "You're sitting pretty close together for talking," then went to the back of the house.

"I'd better go," Mary said.

"I'm sorry, but that's probably best," I said, and the evening quickly came to an end.

Another time while we were driving, Mary pulled over and said to me, "I have something for you." She handed me a little box. Inside was a thin gold bracelet.

"Wow! What is this for?" I asked.

"I saw it and thought of you and wanted you to have it."

"Well, thank you so much." My hand shook a bit as she put it on my wrist.

"To get to know each other a little better, why don't we tell each other our darkest secrets?" Mary suggested.

"Uh, okay, sure."

"I'll start," Mary said. "I'm gay."

I smiled and said, "I figured that!"

"Are you okay with that?"

"Sure! I'm not gay, but it's okay if you are."

We were quiet for a while and then I said, "I am anorexic and bulimarexic."

Mary replied, "I figured you were."

"What made you think that?" I asked, feeling exposed.

"You disappear after every meal, and sometimes I can hear you throwing up."

I was so embarrassed. I didn't know what to say. I sat there in awkward silence until Mary said, "Hey, it's okay. I hope one day you can stop that, but I am here to support you either way."

THE LOVE STORY BEGINS

Several months passed before Mary finally said it. We had hiked up a mountain and when we stopped to catch our breath, she turned around, hugged me, and said, "I am in love with you."

I think my heart skipped a beat. I hugged her back and said, "That's fine! I'm still not gay." (I know, what a ridiculous comeback!)

As she hugged me a little harder and I held on, she said, "Okay, I just needed to tell you."

I stuffed all the feelings I had in that moment as deep as they could go, continuing to ignore my true affections for Mary. I couldn't blend my religious upbringing and my deep connection to her. I usually just lived in my little la-la land and didn't think about it. But I kept thinking, *This is normal. We are really, really good friends. Good friends love each other, Mary knows I'm not gay, and it will all be fine!* I was so confused. I knew I had feelings for Mary, but my church teachings told me she was going to Hell and I would be, too, if I stayed true to my feelings.

Mary didn't seem to have a problem with her sexuality. She would give intimate hugs and back rubs, and I would give them back to her. She would caress me, and I never told her no. I never felt coerced but rather enjoyed the gentle touch, and my love for her grew. I just couldn't tell myself the truth. Feeling guilty after kissing her yet still allowing her to caress me, I just knew I was going to Hell. Even though I kept telling myself I was straight, my actions never matched my words.

One afternoon, Mary and I went to the ball field to hang out. As we parked, I saw my uncle approaching the car. Turning to Mary I said, "He'll smell the beer on my breath" (we had stopped by a brewery for lunch on the way to the field). But after a quick conversation with me, off he went.

When I returned home later that evening, my uncle asked me, "Hey, you got a minute?"

"Sure," I said, with butterflies in my belly.

"I have noticed, since you've lived here, that some of your behaviors are things I didn't know about you before you came."

I felt ice running through my veins and couldn't say anything in response.

"So, I think, based on some of your behaviors, that you need to move out. I can't have that in my house."

I was stunned. The feelings of shame and unworthiness were overwhelming. My heart broke that he didn't want me in his home. Still with my head spinning, I finally responded, "Do you need me to move out right now?"

"No, it's late to do all that. You can sleep here tonight and leave in the morning. Good night."

"Good night."

I watched him go down the hall as I sat frozen on the couch. Eventually, I stood, walked to my room, and began to pack.

A Moment of Grace

I understand that my uncle could do nothing other than what he believed was in the Bible. He was always an awesome person, and it was devastating for me that I disappointed him. I send him love.

THE LOVE STORY BEGINS

Circa 1983

17

Crisis Creates Change

The night my uncle asked me to move out, I didn't sleep at all. Trying to come up with a plan while packing my bags, I thought to myself, *Where will I live? I can't go home. It's too far to drive from Hickory to Boone every day, and I don't have the money to get an apartment on my own.*

Early the next morning, I left for the counselor education office and went into a workroom to wait for Mary. While waiting, I called home and got my dad on the phone. "Daddy, would you be really disappointed if I didn't stay here?"

"What do you mean? Stay where?"

"At graduate school. I don't think I can do it. Can I come home?"

After pausing he said, "Well of course you can come home."

I started to cry. "Okay, I'll call you later."

When Mary came into the office, she asked, "What's wrong? Why are you crying?"

"I'm going to have to go home and quit school. I can't afford to stay here. My uncle was letting me stay rent free, but last night he kicked me out. I called Daddy and he said I could come home."

Mary looked at me and said, "You are not going home. You are going to move in with me."

"How's that going to work? Shelby is there, and there won't be enough room," I said.

"You can sleep on the daybed," Mary countered. "Besides, I really don't think Shelby will be there much longer."

"Well," I said, "you still need to ask her. I don't want to be in the way or cause any trouble."

Mary called and got ahold of Shelby, explaining what was happening. After hanging up, she turned to me and said, "Shelby is fine with it."

That started the awkward living situation between two distant, soon-to-be ex-girlfriends, an unenlightened straight chick, and Sheba.

Shelby seemed very happy that I was there and was very nice, but the tension was incredible. Mary and Shelby would have heated conversations. They never got violent, but in such a small house it was evident that things were not good. Fulfilling my self-inflicted role as a people pleaser, I tried to lighten the mood, but that didn't help at all. Shelby was spending less and less time at the apartment, and Mary and I were often there alone.

One night, while I was sleeping on the daybed, Shelby and Mary were having a heated discussion in the bedroom. All of a sudden, Mary was standing at the daybed asking, "Can you move over?"

"What? Um, yeah," I whispered. "Are you okay?"

"No," Mary said, and started kissing me.

Oh my God, her lips were so warm, and my body started getting all tingly. My brain just disconnected! I started thinking stupid stuff like, *Well this is okay. She needs to be comforted. This isn't gross at all. This is like kissing a guy, except her lips are so soft.*

Barging into the room, Shelby said, "This is stupid."

I sat straight up.

Shelby continued, "If you're going to sleep together, you might as well have the big bed."

"No, it's okay," I stammered.

"Okay, thanks," Mary said as she got up and went to the bedroom, with me scrambling behind her.

I felt horrible. I didn't know what to do with all that had just happened. Mary got into bed, and I could hear Shelby crying in the other room. Mary looked at me, got out of bed, and went out to talk to Shelby. I don't know what they said, but she soon returned to bed.

Shelby moved out soon after that, but before she did, she had us go with her to find her own place. She insisted that I go, which was really uncomfortable. Unfortunately, at the end of the school year, Shelby made the decision to quit school and return home.

Now it was just Mary, Sheba, and me. Feeling guilty, I talked it over with Mary. She emphasized that they were already breaking up and that meeting me had nothing to do with it other than making it happen a little quicker, which she said was a good thing: "I couldn't kick her out, but it was time."

Being that it seems to be part of my DNA, I still felt responsible, but I unpacked my stuff. Mary made room in the dresser and closet, and that was that.

We went back to hiking every weekend, going to school, and visiting her mom and sometimes my family. Her family was way cooler than my family about embracing a new friend and treating them like family, so I loved going to her mom's house on weekends. We would hang out and watch football with her brother, eat homemade pizzas, and drink beer. I loved not having to fear that my uncle would smell it on me and see me as a sinner. Time with Mary's family felt comfortable—until the day when Mary's mom took me up to the attic to talk.

"I don't know what your intentions are," her mom said, "but you better not hurt Mary."

"I don't plan to," I said, feeling my face flush. I was feeling guilty and wasn't sure what I had done.

"Well, you know what just happened with Shelby, and they have been friends a while. Shelby really hurt Mary. Mary is a good girl, and she doesn't deserve to be hurt."

"I really don't plan to hurt her," I said. "She's a very good friend to me, and I don't want to do anything that would ever hurt her. I promise."

"Alright then," her mom said. "I think you are good for her. I haven't seen her this happy in a long time. I just want it to stay that way."

I knew that Mary's mom didn't know that Mary was gay, so she never questioned Mary falling asleep on my lap or the times we spent with each other. When we were alone, Mary and I had an unspoken relationship that went way further than friends. Though the next seven years would test our relationship in ways we could never have imagined, I really believed I would keep my promise.

A Moment of Grace

Mary's love for me has never faltered. She was the only one who saw me—really saw me—the only one who saw the me she knew was truly inside. She saw past the anxiety, the façade, and the denial. She has been, and always will be, the deepest love I have ever known.

Broken Trust

One evening I decided to attend a service at the campground in Blowing Rock, North Carolina, where my siblings and I had attended our church camp. Some of my classmates from Berkshire would be there, and there would be a choir with some BCC students.

Music always opens deep places in my soul. I can start singing or listening to music, and the tears start to flow. So I was excited to reunite with my choir director and some classmates as we joined together to sing that evening. I didn't expect that participating would affect me the way it did.

Singing all the old hymns, being back in that chapel, and being a part of the choir started pulling on the deepest parts of me. I felt so sad. While trying to sing and not cry, I thought about my uncle catching Mary and me sitting close together on the couch and about how he had walked up to the car at the softball field one afternoon when I had beer on my breath. The tears brimmed in my eyes. The shame I felt from my uncle asking me to move out because he felt I was not worthy to live in his home was breaking me apart.

As I looked around the room, I realized that I felt disconnected from everyone. The chapel was full of people I loved, people I had spent wonderful camp times with during my youth. But it felt as though I had grown away from the person I was back then. I couldn't put my finger on it, but I didn't feel like I belonged there anymore.

Believing that God must be condemning me, I felt guilty for liking Mary so much. Even though I was far from telling myself the truth, I felt I was in deep trouble. I really had to fight to stay in control while singing, and apparently I wasn't very convincing. Following the program, one of the adult leaders at the camp approached me and asked if I was okay. I told him I was fine, making up some excuse about missing the old college days.

Mary was expecting me to be home by bedtime, but I decided to stop by my uncle's house first. I had always trusted him, and he was always the cool uncle.

I have always wondered about that decision. Was I purposefully trying to get an external force to make me stay away from Mary? Was I trying to find absolution? Was I hoping that even though he didn't want to smell beer on my breath that my uncle would miraculously find my friendship with Mary to be beautiful and approved by God?

I rang the doorbell, and my uncle came to the door. The butterflies in my stomach were more like elephants stampeding throughout my body as my heart raced and my breath quickened.

I managed to ask, "Do you have a minute to talk?"

"Of course. What's up? Are you alright? Have you been crying?"

"I don't know if I'm alright. I've been crying because at the camp meeting tonight I felt very emotional and have some thoughts that I need to run past you."

"Sure."

"Well—" I started and then couldn't decide what to say. I quickly realized that he wouldn't agree with Mary being a homosexual.

"Never mind. Sorry. I'm expected at Mary's house, and she'll wonder where I am."

"Do you need to call her? Sounds like you really need to talk."

Tears poured down my cheeks.

"What's wrong?"

"Mary's gay!" I blurted out. As my face burned hot, I immediately regretted saying it. I had broken a sacred trust and knew instinctively that I shouldn't have shared her business.

"I figured that," my uncle replied. "You know you need to end the relationship unless she's willing to denounce her homosexuality. Are you a homosexual too?"

"NO!" I practically screamed. "NO, I am not a homosexual, but she is my friend and I want to help her."

"You can't help her, and if you're going to remain friends with her then you're putting yourself at risk. You say you aren't a homosexual, but if you're hanging out with her you're likely going to get pulled into that lifestyle."

My throat closed and my body trembled. All I could get out was a whisper: "I need to go. Thank you for talking with me."

We said our goodbyes and I left for home.

What followed was a very long and anxious trip back to my and Mary's home. This was before cell phones and computers, so I had no way to contact Mary when I left my uncle's house and was in no way willing to stay a second longer. I worried that Mary would wonder where I was. I worried that I wouldn't be able to talk to her when I got back. My stomach was in knots, and I felt like I was going to be sick. I cried throughout the entire drive. I know part of it was the shame and disappointment I felt when I saw my uncle avoid eye contact with me. The other part was that I didn't want to hurt Mary. I had never expected to move until graduation, so the situation with my uncle was gut-wrenching.

The conversation I had with Mary's mom and the promise I had made her then popped into my head. I hated myself in that moment. The suicidal thoughts that always ran close to my consciousness came back in full force. I had always felt like I was unworthy, and that theme was hitting hard now because I was about to tell Mary she was somehow "less than." I was still hiding the fact that I was in love with her, though I didn't know it and always framed every thought with *I love her deeply as a friend*, just like I had loved my inseparable friend Kay in college. I thought about driving off the mountain. *How can I make it look like an accident so no one would know?* Every time I moved closer to the edge I would pull back. Then I became angry at myself that I couldn't even kill myself right! As I battled my mental demons, I got closer and closer to the house. I could barely take a breath.

When I got to the house, Mary was in bed. I let myself in, and Sheba barked. I calmed her and then heard Mary call out from the bedroom, "Are you alright?"

"Yeah, I'm fine." *Dang, I should have used another word.*

Mary got out of bed and came out into the living room. She turned on a light, looked at me, and said, "Really?"

"You are going to hate me," I said sheepishly.

"I could never hate you. What happened?"

I took a deep breath and said, "I got really emotional at the camp meeting tonight."

"Okay. I wondered why you weren't back yet. Do you want to talk about it?"

"Um, I went to talk to Uncle Gordon," I whispered. "That's why I'm late."

"What happened?"

"I told him you were gay."

"Why did you do that?" Mary asked. "That was not your story to tell."

"I know. I am so sorry." Then came a slew of words in one breath: "I don't know, it was the music, and I felt wrong, and I couldn't sing the songs without crying, and I feel so different, and I don't know what is wrong with me, and I wanted to drive off the road and then I didn't want to hurt you, and I think I just need to move out. My uncle thinks I need to move out!"

Tearing up, Mary said, "No, don't do that. I don't want you to do that. It will be okay; it really will be okay."

"How can it be?" I asked. "You're gay, I'm not, and I think I just need to move out. I told my dad earlier that I would come home."

At this point, Mary began to panic. "No, you can't go back there! NO! DON'T DO THIS!" Mary tried to hug me, but I pushed her away.

"No, I can't. I don't know what's wrong with me," I said.

Getting really upset, Mary started to leave the house. I tried to pull her back, but she said, "Let go of me."

"No, don't go!" I yelled as I pushed her back from the door.

She pushed me aside, I grabbed her, and we both rushed to get to the door—me to block it and her to leave. I was terrified.

After Mary made it out the door, I went to call one of the teachers who worked at the counseling clinic. As I was telling her what had happened, how scared I was that Mary had left, and that I didn't know what she was going to do, Mary walked back in. She had clearly been crying.

"Who are you talking to?" she asked.

Feeling the color leave my face and fearing that Mary was going to be really mad, I said, "I called Sherry."

"Put her on the phone," Sherry said over the line.

"She wants to talk to you," I said.

Mary glared at me. "How could you?"

"I was scared you would hurt yourself." I had projected my own suicidal thoughts onto Mary.

Mary got on the phone in the bedroom, and I walked out into the kitchen. Later, she came out and said, "Sherry wants to talk to you."

"Yes?" I said as I took the phone from Mary.

"Can you stay there tonight and be safe?" she asked.

"Yes."

"Mary has agreed to stay at home and see me in the morning. If you have any problems, call me back."

I hung up the phone and stayed sitting on the floor.

Mary walked in and said, "You didn't have to call her. I just needed some space. I wasn't going to hurt myself. Now I have to see her in the morning, or I'm going to be committed."

I felt like an ass. I couldn't look at her and didn't know what to do. "I'm so sorry," I whispered. "I just didn't know what to do, and I never wanted to hurt you. I do love you."

"I love you too," Mary said. "I never wanted to hurt you either."

We hugged.

"Do you need me to sleep on the daybed?" Mary asked.

"No," I said, "If anyone needs to, it's me."

"No, come to bed. Let's get some sleep."

And with that, we climbed into bed. I always slept on my stomach, with my right arm down with my palm facing up. Without fail, it would land under Mary's hand, and we would fall asleep that way. That night was no different. Tears rolled down my face as I felt the warmth of her hand and the love I had for her. I still couldn't admit to myself that I was in love with her because of what I had been taught in youth group and by Paw Paw and my uncle: homosexuals are an abomination, all homosexuals are damned into the lake of fire for eternity, and if you go along with the sin you are a sinner.

The next morning, we were both quiet. When I asked if she needed me to go with her to see Sherry, she said, "Yes, Sherry would probably want that."

We didn't speak as we drove into town. When we got to the clinic, Sherry came out, nodded to me, and asked Mary to go back to the office with her.

After about an hour, Sherry came out and asked me, "Do you need to talk with me?"

"No, I'm fine," I said. I glanced up and Mary caught my eye and smiled, shaking her head. "No, really, I'm okay. Thank you," I said while avoiding direct eye contact with Sherry.

When we got back to the car, Mary said, "I know what you did was out of concern for me. Thank you."

"I am still so sorry!"

"I do need to ask a favor," she said.

"Yes, whatever you need." (I have since learned to say to people, "I will do it if I can.")

Mary continued, "I had to promise Sherry that I would have someone with me this weekend. I'm going to invite my mom up and, to avoid questions about where you are and why you're not here, can you hang out with us? I thought we'd go on a hike or something."

"Yes," I said. "I can do that."

I was glad to help Mary out, but it was also awkward for me and Mary to spend time with her mom and act as if the proverbial elephant wasn't in the room. Mary's mom didn't seem to know the difference, and if she did, she didn't say anything. Mary and I knew that we were not ourselves.

The weekend came and went. We got up on Monday and got ready for class. Our futures still loomed in front of us. "Are you going to move out?" asked Mary.

"I don't want to," I said, "but I don't know what to do."

"Well, it's up to you," said Mary. "I don't want you to go, but if you can't live with me, then you need to go."

That hit me hard. I didn't want to go. My brain started spinning again. If I stayed I would be sinning by living with a gay person, and if I left I wouldn't be able to afford to stay at grad school and would have to move home with my parents. I loved graduate school and Mary, and I couldn't bear the thought of leaving her.

"You okay?" asked Mary.

"Uh, yeah, just trying to figure out what to do."

"You don't have to decide right now. We need to go."

We left for class and then met up for lunch, avoiding any deep conversation. We made it through the day, and I don't recall ever talking about it again.

I knew that I didn't want to live without Mary, even though I still couldn't figure out why. So I stayed. Our connection continued to deepen as we went through our daily lives. Time with Mary always left me feeling safe and loved, and I looked forward to the two upcoming years that we would be together.

A Moment of Grace

I never wanted to hurt Mary, and breaking her sacred trust broke her heart. I can't believe she didn't walk away from me then. Never have I found a greater love than the love of Mary. People joke about how long she waited for me. Her waiting for me helped me heal, and I will be forever grateful.

19

GRE

As the date neared for me to take the graduate record exam to stay in grad school, I became a bundle of nerves—I had never been a good test taker. My advisor assured me that I would do well because I was proving that I could do graduate work and had been getting good grades thus far.

The exam was divided into three parts, and it was random which three parts each student was given. It was either two parts math and one part English or two parts English and one part math. I hoped that I would receive the two English packets because I suck at math. All through elementary, middle, and high school, I never understood it. Teachers would explain it to me ad nauseam and, just when I would think I was getting a grasp on a concept, they would walk away from me, leaving me at a loss once more. So when I received my packet with two parts math and one part English, my heart sank.

Feeling defeated before even starting the exam, I willed myself not to run out of the room. I opened the English packet and started the test, which I had three hours to complete. I felt fairly confident about the English section, although the way the questions were asked was very tricky and confusing. When I got to the math part, it was horrible! I tried to keep my mind open and process the equations slowly, but it didn't really matter because I just didn't understand it. I didn't even know how to answer over half of the questions, so I chose the letter C throughout most of the math portion. If I had a reasonable guess, I would pick it. Once I had gone through the whole exam, I went back to some of the ones I had answered and reviewed them again to see if I had a better choice the second time. I used up the entire allotted time trying to get the right answers.

Mary was waiting for me when I was done. Seeing the look on my face, she said, "I have an idea. Get in my car."

My brain cells were drained, and I did as she told me without asking any questions. She drove away from the campus and out onto the parkway, then turned onto a small road and drove until we found a place to pull the car off to the side. We got out and I looked around and asked, "What are we doing here?"

Mary opened the trunk and pulled out a blanket and a cooler. "Let's go," she said.

We walked up a hill and went to a flat section of grass. Mary spread out the blanket and opened the cooler. "Here," she offered.

After I accepted the beer that was in her hand, she pulled out some snacks. I reached over and hugged her.

"Thank you," I said. "This is really nice."

"Just rest," she said. "You can sleep, you can talk, you can look at the sky—whatever you need to do."

I was so exhausted physically and emotionally.

In silence, we drank our beers and ate some snacks. As I lay down and looked up at the sky, I noticed it was a bright Carolina blue color with puffy white clouds. The October air was perfect—cool and crisp without being too cold—and that moment was perfect. I lay back on the blanket and closed my eyes, feeling the warmth of the sun on my face and the cool breeze on my skin.

I was awakened by Mary calling my name. "Midge, come on sleepyhead. Midge, wake up."

As I looked up, I saw the sky was less brilliant and the clouds were now wispy. I stretched and looked up at Mary. "What time is it?" I asked.

"It's about 4:30," she said.

"Oh my gosh, I'm sorry!"

"Don't apologize. You needed the rest."

"I don't think I passed the exam."

"You don't know that. You probably did better than you think."

"Oh, I doubt that!" I exclaimed. "I guessed on most of it. It had two parts math!"

"Uh oh," Mary said, knowing that math was not my strong suit. "Well, what's done is done."

I don't recall how long it was before the test results came back. I remember I fretted the whole time, knowing that if I failed I would have to leave graduate school. Finally, I was called to set up an appointment with my advisor. When I went to her office, Dr. G. welcomed me in and smiled.

"How are you doing, Midge?" she asked.

I squirmed in my chair and said, "I'm fine, thanks."

"Good. You're sure doing well in your classes from what I can tell. Are you enjoying them?" she asked.

OMG, I thought, *just tell me! This is killing me!*

"Yes," I replied with a smile.

"Good!" she said. "I received your GRE results and wanted to go over some options with you."

I stopped breathing.

"So, I'll just get right to it. You failed."

OH GOD OH GOD OH GOD, I kept screaming in my head, though I said nothing out loud.

Dr. G. looked at me and smiled. "I'm sorry," she continued, "I know this is not the news you wanted to hear. Had you thought you did well?"

I cleared my throat and said, "No, I didn't think I did well but was hoping I hadn't failed. What happens now?"

"Well, you cannot be admitted to graduate school with a failing score."

"Oh, no," I whispered. "I don't know what I'll do if I don't stay in graduate school. I definitely want to be here."

"Well, the thing you have in your favor is that you have been here and are doing the work. So you have three options: you can leave graduate school, you can retake the test—"

"NO!" I interrupted, "I cannot do that again!"

Dr. G. smiled and said, "I understand, and I wouldn't advise it. The standard deviation of error for the GRE is 30 points, and you failed it by 30 points! It's basically impossible for you to retake the test and make up that number of points."

"Especially if I get two parts math again!" I said.

"Yes, that did seem to be a huge part of the problem."

"What's the third option?" I asked.

"I can go before the review board and tell them that you're a good student who's doing a great job in the classes and understands the content of the work but is just a bad test taker."

"Let's do that!" I responded.

"I can't promise anything," Dr. G said, "but I will be glad to give it a try. I really believe you belong here and that you'll be successful in your goals."

Again, I can't tell you how long it took to get a response from Dr. G. I was working in the counseling office one day when she walked in.

"Midge, glad you're here. Are you busy?" she asked as she headed to her office.

"No," I replied.

"Come in," she said, opening her office door.

We sat down in her tiny office, which had barely enough room for us to sit opposite each other without touching knees. When she closed the door, I felt all the air leave the room. I watched her as she settled in and unpacked her briefcase, distracting myself by looking at all the books on the shelves, pictures of her with people I didn't know, and her desk full of papers, coffee mugs, and envelopes. It was a welcome diversion from what I was afraid to hear.

"Well then," she said, bringing me back into the moment, "I have some news."

"Okay," I said.

"They agreed."

"What? They agreed that I can stay?" I asked, getting my hopes up.

"Yes!" she said. "With one condition."

"Oh no, what's the condition?"

"You'll be on a provisional basis for the rest of your time in graduate school. If you make one C in any class you take while you're here, you'll be dismissed from the graduate program and won't be allowed to reapply."

We stared at each other, and then Dr. G. broke the silence. "Do you agree with those terms?"

"Yes, uh, I guess," I answered.

"Well, you need to be sure."

"I just wonder if I can do it."

"There will be some challenging courses," she warned, "but I think you can do it. Unless you just want to leave now, I suggest you at least try."

"Yes, of course I will," I declared.

Mary was thrilled that I was given a second chance. We celebrated that night with a special dinner, talking by the warmth of the oil lamp on the table, with Sheba snoring beside us. I took in the moment and really loved everything about it. I felt accepted, loved, and cared for by Mary, and Sheba was getting used to me and I loved having a dog's energy around. I never wanted that moment to end. I had never felt so good.

> ### A Moment of Grace
>
> I have always doubted my abilities and my intelligence. Educational testing is not geared toward innate abilities. I am grateful that Dr. G. saw my potential and found a way to keep me in school. I hope that one day the system will change, and I am learning that being average does not take away my talents and gifts.

20

Life Emerging

After my meeting with Dr. G., October flew by. My routine of attending classes, studying, and hiking on the weekends continued. I adore the mountains and hiking, so I was in bliss most of the time.

The most challenging part was my family's expectation that I would come home every weekend. This was the same old pattern, stemming from Momma and Daddy's disappointment that I hadn't attended ASU for my undergraduate degree. I had no interest in going home every weekend, as it was more beneficial to spend time away from school with Mary. My family had no clue as to why I would want to spend so much time with her. It isn't like she was someone I was in a relationship with—she wasn't a boyfriend—so why would I want to hang out that much with someone who was just a friend? But why would they have had a clue? There was no way for them to understand; I didn't understand it myself! I always felt a great deal of guilt when I would tell my parents that I couldn't come home for a weekend and then go with Mary to see her mom instead.

That year, Mary's family invited me to spend Thanksgiving with them. Of course, my family expected me to spend all holidays with them, so the pull of expectations, emotions, and trying to please everyone went on for years. I knew that Mary wanted me to be with her family and that I wanted me to be with them, but my parents would play the guilt card of "Why don't you want to spend time with your own family?" It really was unbearable because I hated hurting my family's feelings. I knew that anything I did, any time I spent with Mary, would anger my parents. I didn't mean to hurt their feelings, but I inevitably always did.

Looking back, I wonder if my parents' anger was a way to mask their hurt and disappointment. I wish I knew then what I know now. I wish I could have been honest with myself and my family.

I made the decision to go home for Thanksgiving but told Mary I would try to be at her house by late afternoon. Her mother, bless her little heart, told Mary that they would hold dinner for me. I didn't want her to do that, but Mary said, "It doesn't matter what time we eat. We eat Thanksgiving dinner late because we watch football. Just get there as soon as you can."

That was easier said than done. Even though my parents ate around noon, they expected me to be home and stay home through the duration of Thanksgiving break. I kept watching the clock, chewing fast, and trying to look like I was paying attention to the conversations being had around me. All I wanted to do was go see Mary.

After the meal was cleaned up, I packed my things so I could hit the road. My parents were not happy. They continued to challenge my decision and question me about why I had any interest in going to see someone else's family. Thanksgiving, they implied, was family time—and Mary was not my family.

While they were berating me, I thought, *Stay home and do what? Watch Daddy watching football and Momma reading a book while my brother was outside?* Polly and her husband didn't live near my parents, so they didn't come home for Thanksgiving, and I thought that was okay because husbands get to make those decisions and my sister didn't have a choice.

Amid my parents' irrational feelings of anger toward me, I told them that I loved them and that I would call them later. With that, I left to go to Mary's house.

When I got to Mary's home in Cary, North Carolina, I was welcomed with open arms, wagging tails, and the sound of football on TV. Mary's mom handed me a beer, encouraged me to put my things up in the bedroom, and come down when I was ready. Mary grabbed my bag and went upstairs with me to her childhood bedroom. Her bed and dresser were dark mahogany wood with white dresser knobs, her walls were lavender, and she had a floral lavender-print bedspread. It was all much more girly than I would have imagined. I finally took a deep breath. It felt good being there.

Mary hugged me and told me how glad she was that I was there. After Mary and I talked for a while, her mom showed up at the door saying, "You girls coming down? The game is getting good, and it's almost time to eat."

"Yes," Mary said.

I wanted to stay up there a while longer.

The rest of the evening was amazing—laughter, great football, a wonderful home-cooked meal, and the feeling of acceptance. Her brother, Joe, was there with his dog, Cracker. Mary's mom lived with Joe's other dog, CJ, and then there was Sheba. Mary's mom was totally fine with dogs being in the house, unlike my mom who never allowed that until Polly got her a Sheltie for the first time. The visit was wonderful! We ate way too much and screamed for the teams we wanted to win. It was nice to feel relaxed and free of judgment and to just be myself.

The next day, we went out to pick up a Christmas tree and that evening had a tree decorating party, complete with Brandy Alexanders.

I had never had those, but they were yummy; they are made with ice cream, Kahlua, brandy, and crème de cacao. I wasn't vegan then and loved the amazing food and that delicious beverage. Unfortunately, I was still in the deep cycle of anorexia/bulimarexia. I thought I had hidden it well, but I later learned that Mary's mom was concerned (of course Mary already knew).

After Thanksgiving break, Mary and I headed back to finish up the last part of the semester before Christmas break. I was already scheming how to work out the holidays so that I could spend as much time with Mary as possible.

The holidays turned out to be the most emotionally exhausting part of my year. I tried to make everyone happy, not to disappoint anyone, and to act like I was present and having fun, all while watching the clock and trying not to make people hurry. My insides were churning through all the stress. I was never successful. Mary understood what I was going through and still wanted me to celebrate with her and her family, but my parents expected me to be home as soon as the semester broke for Christmas and stay home until the next semester started. Though Mary hoped I could spend all my time with her family, she knew that wasn't realistic. Her next hope was that I could get to her mom's house at least by Christmas evening.

While we were in graduate school, I almost always made it to Mary's house by late afternoon or evening for all the holidays. By the time I would get to her mom's house, I was emotionally drained. I felt guilty, shamed, selfish, and like a horrible daughter for leaving my family. In my wake, I left a very wounded and angry family that couldn't understand why I was choosing to do what I was doing, and I couldn't explain it to them. The worst part is that they put the blame on Mary and kept telling me that she shouldn't have that much control over me. I would tell them this was something I really wanted to do, but it was all a broken record—same story, different day. To this day, I still feel the pressure of needing to please everyone and not being able to.

But there was something that could please me. It involved Mary, of course, and a dream of mine that I hadn't shared with her.

A Moment of Grace

I understand parents want their children at home for the holidays. I have never had children, but I am sure it would hurt me if my kids didn't come home. My parents may never understand why I had to break away in the manner I did. I am sad for the pain it caused them.

21

Dani

In the community of Boone, North Carolina, there was a periodical called the *I WANNA* that sold all kinds of stuff—from seeds to boats, farm animals to houses, and anything else you could imagine. If there was something you wanted, you could find it in the *I WANNA*! On one particular day, as I scanned its pages, I saw an ad that read "Puppies for Sale!" Labrador puppies. I wanted one.

Showing the ad to Mary, I said, "Look at this listing. I would really love to go check these puppies out. I've always dreamed of having a Labrador retriever."

"What would you do with it? We're in class, and I am not going to have another Jo Jo."

"I'll train it."

"Where is it going to stay?"

"I can put it in the bathroom."

"All day?"

"I can tie it outside."

Let me pause to say that I was raised in a home where our dogs were never allowed in the house; they roamed free or were on a chain until my dad finally got a fence. Tying a dog outside was a perfectly reasonable suggestion to me, although Mary didn't like it.

"Can't we just go look?" I asked.

"We can go look," Mary consented.

"I've already picked out a name."

"Oh God!" Mary exclaimed. "What if it doesn't work out? I thought we were only going to look."

"I know, but just in case. I will name her 'Noble's Danielle Colleen.'"

"That's quite a name."

"Dani, for short."

"Sounds like you have it all worked out!"

As it happened, the puppies were in Hickory, North Carolina—my birthplace.

When Mary saw the address, she asked, "Do you want to stop by your parents' house?"

"Absolutely not."

We pulled up to a rundown mobile home with a dog lot in the backyard where the puppy and its mother were. It was a muddy lot, and the water in the one dog bowl was filthy. There were also several kids with dirty diapers and marks on their backs running around the yard.

The owner came out and asked, "Are you here about that dog?"

"Yes, can we take her out?"

"Yeah." He grabbed the puppy by the scruff of the neck, pulled it out of the dog lot, and tried to put a rope around its neck. The puppy started lunging away from the rope.

I picked up the puppy and it calmed down. Mary came over and petted it, and I could see in her eyes that we were taking this baby home.

"Is that the momma?" I asked.

"Yeah."

"Where's the daddy?"

"Not here."

"Is he about the same size as the momma?"

"Naw, he's about 110 pounds. She's about 60."

"Wow!"

I pretended to check her out, knowing all along she wasn't staying there. "I think she will work out fine," I said to the owner. "Is the momma for sale?"

I saw Mary's shocked expression as the man said, "Naw. Paperwork is inside."

The home was as dirty as I had expected, and I was happy to be getting that puppy out of that situation. I also wished I could have taken her momma too!

When we got to the car, I said to Mary, "I'm going to hold her so she won't be afraid."

"Okay. Get in and I'll hand her to you when you're set."

I got in, buckled up, and she placed the puppy in my lap before getting into the driver's seat and looking over at me.

I smiled and petted Dani, and dust flew up from her body. "She needs a bath!" I said.

"Yes, she does!" Mary agreed.

When Mary started the engine, Dani dove from my lap, between the front seats, and onto the floorboard behind the driver's seat.

"Just leave her," Mary said. "She's fine."

Dani stayed on the floor all the way back up to Boone.

Back at home, it took three baths to clean Dani up. That night, we went to watch Mary play softball. Dani was so small that she curled up in between my feet as I stood to watch the game.

I started training Dani right away. With a father who weighed 100 pounds, she had the potential to be a big Labrador, and I wanted to make sure that I had control over her behavior and that she was a good, responsible, and safe dog to go out into the community—not a Jo Jo. Dani proved to be very smart, and she quickly learned to heel, sit, stay, and come. She did exceptionally well with potty training and didn't soil the house as long as we paid close attention and got her out regularly. She wasn't quite yet ready to be left alone in the house without supervision, though, so on long class days I would tie her up outside—only to come home and find that I would need to fill in all the holes that she had dug up for amusement throughout the day.

One chilly night, when Mary had a late softball game, she suggested that we try keeping Dani in the house with Sheba (it was too cold to take the dogs to the game). We had tried it a few times and it had gone well, so we left Dani and Sheba together in the apartment while I went to watch Mary's game. The thing that set this time apart from other times was that we had put some flea spray on the dogs before we left. This was back in the day when they used toxic chemicals to treat fleas, and the only options available were flea dips, flea collars, and flea sprays. We put some flea spray on them about an hour before we left and didn't think anything about it.

When we came back from the softball game, Mary looked in through the window and started laughing.

"What?" I asked as I started moving toward the door. "What's so funny?"

Mary turned to me and said, "Now, don't be upset. It's really okay. Don't be upset."

I pushed past her, looked inside the door, and exclaimed, "Oh my God! She's in so much trouble," assuming that it was Dani who did what I was looking at since Sheba had never done anything like this. As I looked through the door, I saw a mound of debris in the middle of the room. When I say a mound, I'm talking about a pile of stuff that was about my height, about 5'7".

"Don't be mad," Mary repeated. "It's gonna be okay. It's gonna be fine."

"It is NOT fine!" I said emphatically.

All I could think of was that Jo Jo Jr. had come on board and that Mary would one day talk about me and the bad dog I had brought into her house. I couldn't believe that Mary didn't seem to be upset at all and actually thought it was funny!

After we went into the house and walked past the mound to get the dogs to take them out to the bathroom, Mary said, "I really believe it's because we put that spray on them. They must have just run through the house and had fun."

When we got back inside and started dismantling the pile, we were amazed at how much had been disrupted and pulled into this mountain of mess! There was the horsehair backing that had been under the carpet, as well as the carpet itself, all in a big heap. The side chair and coffee table from the living room were up against the carpet, and on and under all of that were books, magazines, coasters, wood from the basket next to the stove, and shoes! A glass ashtray that had been on the coffee table was all the way across the room next to the stove. I about freaked out!

Mary kept saying, "It's okay. We can put it all back. I don't think anything is messed up."

Holding up a coaster that had been chewed on, I defiantly said, "What about this?"

"Jo Jo did that," Mary replied.

As we continued to clean up and put things back, we were amazed to discover that nothing had been broken! The glass ashtray wasn't even chipped. I couldn't believe it. The only thing that had been pulled apart was some of the horsehair backing from underneath the carpet.

Dani and Sheba must have rolled around and did all the things that dogs do to get a scent off themselves. I imagined the amount of chaotic energy that Dani and Sheba had as they exploded through the room after we left. To get that carpet all the way into the middle of the room, they had to have clawed, dragged, and pushed it while tearing through the house with such force! I heaved a big sigh of relief.

Mary and I promised each other that we would never, ever put that spray on them again unless we could be with them until the scent was not so overwhelming.

Dani was an amazing fur kid. She was my best companion, won her companion dog title in obedience, and played Sandy in the High Point production of *Annie* and Belle in *The Miracle Worker*. I sure miss that girl.

> ### A Moment of Grace
>
> As Maya Angelou once said to Oprah Winfrey, "You did in your 20s what you knew how to do. And when you knew better, you did better."[3] I pray for all animals who are mistreated, and I give myself grace for not knowing how to report animal abuse at that time.

---

[3] "The Powerful Lesson Maya Angelou Taught Oprah," OWN, Oprah's Life Class, originally aired October 19, 2011, https://www.oprah.com/oprahs-lifeclass/the-powerful-lesson-maya-angelou-taught-oprah-video.

If it's not about love,

it's not about God.

—THE MOST REV. MICHAEL B CURRY,
27TH PRESIDING BISHOP OF
THE EPISCOPAL CHURCH

Rebirth

Part 4

Life after Graduate School

Mary and I continued to live together all through graduate school. We loved hiking with Dani and Sheba, who had become the best of friends. I supported Mary at her softball games, and she supported me when I was the goalie for the intramural soccer team. Our lives were so intertwined that we were a couple without officially being one.

As we were approaching the end of graduate school, I began to have the same feelings I had when I was leaving college—the ones of dread at the prospect of saying goodbye to Kay. Mary assured me that this would be different and we would remain friends, but neither of us could predict the future, and we knew it.

Mary's father softened the blow by gifting Mary with his car and all his camping gear so she could drive to California and Washington to visit her paternal aunts and maternal grandparents. Mary immediately turned to me and said, "Will you go with me?"

"Sleep in a tent all the way across the country?"

"Yes, doesn't that sound like fun?"

"It sounds more fun than boot camp!"

"It'll be a lot more fun than that!"

I felt very anxious about the trip, but I wanted more time with Mary. We started making plans as to what route we would take and the places to stop and see along the way. MapQuest became our friend and Mary had a ball planning it all out.

Graduation day was bittersweet. I was thrilled that I was finished studying for exams, yet every time I thought about leaving Mary, I felt a lump come into my throat, I felt sick to my stomach, and my heart hurt. Though I was excited about the trip, I was also apprehensive about it. I really wanted to go, but I was scared to death that I wouldn't be able to handle it or that something bad would happen. My thoughts raced with made-up worries: *What if Mary and I wind up hating each other or she figures out that we really aren't compatible? What if I hate camping across the country and don't want to do it once we're too far to turn back?* I never said a word as Mary and I packed up our things, had our families up to toast our accomplishments, closed the apartment, and headed onward to our new adventure.

We spent the first night at Mary's childhood home, as her mom had agreed to keep Dani and Sheba while we were gone. We both hated leaving them behind. The next day Mary and I embarked on what turned out to be a month-long journey. Telling you everything that happened on that trip would be an entire memoir to itself! We survived a swarm of locusts in Lebanon, Tennessee; almost lost our vinyl tent in Texas because of high winds; nearly froze to death at Red Rock, New Mexico, as the 95-degree temperature plummeted to 30 degrees; experienced a surprise snow storm at Mt. Rushmore; had a bear visit our Yosemite campsite; slept on rocks in Colorado Springs when my air mattress deflated; and realized in Kentucky that Mary without coffee is not a pretty picture. I really shouldn't have been left in charge of trying to work the gas camp stove! On the upside, I loved meeting Mary's family and felt at home when I met them.

After the trip, one of the schools I had applied to in Elkin City contacted me for an interview, and I was hired. Although we celebrated, I felt sad that we wouldn't be together anymore. Mary had some interviews lined up, but she was planning to live at her home with her mother, and I would be hours away from her. I couldn't imagine life without Mary. The impact on Dani and Sheba was palpable as well. We spent weekends together, but when Mary would leave, Dani wouldn't play with her ball as often, and Sheba would go and hide under Mary's bed. When they were reunited, they played nonstop.

Mary turned down a job in Rocky Mount and took one in Asheboro because it was closer to Elkin. For the next two years, we saw each other on weekends and vacations. We made it work, but neither of us was happy. During this time, I knew that I was too emotionally connected to Mary, but I wouldn't allow myself to figure out why. I couldn't shake the religious messages of "hellfire for homosexuals." Regrettably, Mary and I prayed for her salvation and for her to be free of her sin.

My job in Elkin City started out well. The previous school counselor had become the principal and wanted to hire someone who would focus on classroom guidance lessons and individual sessions with the students. She talked about the testing program at the school, and I explained that I had issues with math and wouldn't be a good fit if I had to be the test coordinator. She assured me that I wouldn't be required to do that because she would continue to do it.

I loved working with the teachers and students. I did weekly guidance lessons for each class and enjoyed the individual sessions with the students who needed to work through some specific issues. Unfortunately, I was tasked with calculating test scores to identify placement for students in the Exceptional Children's program and, during a meeting, the school psychologist discovered a miscalculation on my part.

The principal glared at me while the psychologist said, "That's why we meet as a team—to catch errors before it's too late."

The following year I was transferred to the high school and my former principal had now become superintendent. At the end of that school year, the principal at the high school called me in for my performance evaluation. It was excellent, but he informed me that my contract would not be renewed for the fall.

"What?"

The principal started to reread his previous statement from a 4×6 index card.

"I heard what you said, I don't understand why."

"I am not at liberty to say. You can opt to quit or your contract will not be renewed."

"So, I'd be fired."

"In a manner of speaking."

Following the meeting, I immediately called Mary.

"I'm out of a job."

"What happened?"

"Remember the principal who hired me and then became superintendent of schools and had me transferred to the high school this year?"

"Of course I remember."

"Well, I just had my performance evaluation, which was excellent, but he said my contract would not be renewed for the fall."

"How can they do that? What reason did he give you?"

"He said he was not at liberty to say, but if I don't resign I will be terminated. Five other new employees have said they were told that too."

"That doesn't sound legal."

"I called Raleigh, and they said that since I wasn't tenured they can legally do it. I'm going to resign because I don't know what they'll put in my file, but then I'm out of a job. I'll have to go home until I figure something out."

"You are not returning home. You will come live with me."

"But I don't have a job!"

"You'll find one. There are schools here, too, you know!"

Once again, Mary found a way for us to stay together. I still felt broken and confused, but at least we would all be together again.

Nevertheless, the next two years would involve a huge twist that I never saw coming.

A Moment of Grace

The previous school counselor, who became the principal and hired me, seemed to like me in the beginning. My inability to do math, which she knew when she hired me, became an issue. She also seemed to have issues with how well the teachers and students bonded with me. Whatever problems the principal had with me, I learned later that she died of a brain tumor. I hope she resolved her own internal struggles before that happened.

23

Out of the Darkness

Moving to Asheboro was like arriving at an oasis in the desert. Mary welcomed me into her home with open arms.

"I want you to feel that this is your home too. You can change the furniture around and make any changes that will make this yours."

"That's really nice of you."

"There's only one thing that can't be changed."

"What's that?"

"Sheba's picture above the mantel has to stay there."

"She is the Queen," I said as we both smiled and nodded our heads.

Mary gave me time to grieve the loss of my job. She told me I would find a job but that there was no reason to look right then. I felt bad about not pulling my weight, yet I was emotionally spent. I would either numb out watching TV or sleep for most of the day before getting up and making some dinner before Mary got home from work. I couldn't begin to think about working again, especially not in a school setting.

Toward the end of that first month living with Mary, she came home and said, "Have you thought about what you want to do next?"

"Not really. I don't know if I could work in a school setting again."

"What about at the mental health center?"

"I was trained in the school counseling tract."

"I don't think that would matter. Give it a try."

I set up an interview, but it went horribly wrong.

"How did it go?" Mary asked when I returned home.

"I was told I don't have enough clinical experience to work in child therapy."

"I bet that was horrible. I'm sorry. You really are good with kids. Maybe the school system here will be better for you," she assured.

"Yeah, okay. I will look into it."

I figured Mary was ready for me to start pulling my weight, and I felt guilty for wanting to retreat back to the couch and never work again. Since I had just left one, I set up an interview at a high school.

I didn't get the job and my self-worth crashed. I was crying when Mary got home, and she hugged me and listened as I ranted, "I shouldn't have moved here. I'm not pulling my weight and I can't find a job and it's all a big mess!"

"None of that is true. It will work out; just give it some time."

As she held me, I cried, "I don't have time. I need a job!"

Later that week I was contacted by an elementary school where the principal was the husband of the high school principal that didn't hire me. I felt uncomfortable but went to the interview.

"Welcome to New Market School. I am Principal Rick. My wife called me right after your interview with her and said, 'Rick, you better hire this girl! She is perfect, not for high school because they will chew her up and spit her out, but she is perfect for you.'"

I felt my cheeks blushing as we continued the interview.

He hired me on the spot, and I became an itinerant school counselor for New Market and Tabernacle Elementary while Mary was a counselor at the mental health center. We fell back into the groove of being roommates. Dani and Sheba were thrilled to be reunited, and we resumed our weekend activities of hiking, camping, and loving life. At least, I thought we were.

At some point, Mary had started acting sad and didn't seem to be the same energetic person I had come to know. We talked about it one day, and Mary revealed that she may be depressed. She found a therapist and started sessions. I thought at the time that things were going to be fine. I had no reason to believe that we wouldn't continue to live together, until one day when Mary came home and said, "I'm gay, I have always been gay, and I will always be gay. I can't live with you anymore because I am still in love with you."

A chill went up my spine and my breath quickened. "I want the name of your therapist," I demanded.

"Why?"

"Because what you just said scared the shit out of me and I have to know why."

Mary gave me the contact information for her therapist but cautioned that she may not take me as a client due to a conflict of interest. I contacted the therapist anyway and explained the situation: "I am Mary's roommate and I need to find out if I'm gay." I told her what had happened, and she asked to talk with Mary, who I then heard telling the therapist that she was fine if I had individual sessions with her.

At my first session I told the therapist, "I'm here to find out if I'm gay. But if I am, I will have to kill myself because I know I will go to Hell for it, and I won't wait around."

The therapist replied with a smile, "I hate working with counselors; y'all know exactly what to say to avoid a commitment."

And with that I started my journey of exploration, which included the therapist's suggestion to go to Metropolitan Community Church to explore homosexuality and the Bible, an idea I initially balked at. "You want me to go to a church with a gay minister to find out if it would be okay with God to be gay? That's nuts! Of course she would say it's okay, she's gay!"

"Just give it a try," she said with a smile. "I think you'll get a lot out of it."

The first time I showed up at Pastor Tina's very small office, I noticed it had a couch with blankets, clothes, and a pillow on it. I froze as I walked through the door, once again remembering lessons from my youth group. Pastor Tina just smiled and said, "Excuse the mess. I slept here last night after seeing a person in crisis. It was too late to go home, and I haven't had a minute to clean up."

"Oh, no problem," I lied.

After Pastor Tina asked me why I was there and how she could help, I gave her the same response I had given my therapist. Her eyebrows went up as she said, "I don't think you will go to hell. I also need you to be honest with me if you are ever feeling suicidal."

"I'm always suicidal," I stated. "I just don't have a plan or the intent to kill myself right now because I don't know if I'm gay."

Pastor Tina looked at me seriously and said, "Tell me if that changes, because the last thing I want is for you to die without knowing how much God loves the you he created."

I agreed to break the awkward moment, and after that we had a very interesting conversation. She gave some background on certain Bible verses that I had never been taught. She also taught a homosexuality and the Bible class that she thought would be good for me to attend and invited me to church, saying, "It's just down this road past the office, in the woods."

Oh great, I thought. *A church in the woods with a lot of gay people. What could go wrong?* "I'll think about it," I said.

"Your friend can come, too, if she's interested. You may feel more comfortable."

When I went home, I talked to Mary about my experience, telling her that I was interested in going to that class and maybe church. "Do you want to come too?" I asked.

"NO," Mary flatly said. "I don't need a group to tell me I'm okay."

I was disappointed that she didn't want to come, but it didn't stop me from filling her in on the things I learned about the "clobber verses" in the Bible that are used to condemn homosexuality. The sad thing is that those verses have been misinterpreted and used against homosexuals, but none of them in context are really condemning same-sex, loving relationships or people who are born biologically LGBTQIA+ individuals.

Even with this support, I struggled with my religious beliefs and what I was being told. *What if gay people just want to believe they're okay?* I thought. *What if it is still a sin?* Battling this issue consumed me, and my eating disorder continued to wreak havoc on my body.

Mary was still dealing with being in love with me and living with me. I knew she was giving me the space to figure things out, but she was struggling. She came home one day and said, "I've applied for a job in Spokane, Washington."

"Really? Oh my God! Are you moving?"

"We'll see if I get the job."

My heart sank while I said, "Your grandparents will be thrilled if you moved there."

"What about you? How would you feel if I moved there?"

"Well, I would miss you, you know that, but you have to do what you have to do."

"You're right."

My heart sank again.

After Mary went to the interview, she called to tell me some important news: "I got the job."

I forced myself to say, "Oh my God! Congratulations! Wow!"

"Thank you," Mary said quietly.

"Are you going to take it?"

"I haven't decided. How are things going there?"

"Okay. I'm taking the wallpaper off the bathroom wall."

"WHY? We rent the house, and we don't have permission to do that."

"Well, it was coming up on the corner and I just started pulling it and, well, it's not going to go back up. It's really old, but maybe I could put stencils up."

"We'll talk about it when I get home."

Mary came back, and I continued to struggle. She turned down the job, and when I asked her why, she said, "It's just not the right time."

I had just turned 30, and Mary and I had known each other for seven years. I was still going to Metropolitan Community Church and still struggling to fully embrace my sexuality. One night, I was sitting in the back pew feeling extremely emotional after Pastor Tina had given a great sermon. On the outside I presented myself as I always did, yet inside I felt out of balance. When the last hymn, "It is Well with My Soul," started, I lost it. I began sobbing uncontrollably to the point that I was struggling to breathe. I clutched my body and rocked while the sobs continued and I kept thinking, *Oh my God, I am gay. I am really gay.* As the song ended, I tried to pull myself together. Several people around me smiled, touched my arm, and asked if I was okay. Embarrassed, I avoided eye contact and said, "I'm fine."

Just then, Pastor Tina came up to the pew and said, "I need some help in a minute, can you hang out?"

"Yeah, sure," I answered.

When she returned, she sat down on the pew and said, "Looked like you were dealing with some pretty heavy feelings tonight."

"Yeah."

"Want to talk about it?"

The tears started to flow again as I whispered, "I think I'm gay." The tears got heavier as Pastor Tina put her hand on my arm.

"You are going to be okay. God loves you."

I kept my head down and tried to get a hold of myself. I hate crying in front of people.

"Listen, a bunch of us are going out to eat. Come join us."

"Thanks, but I should get home. Mary is waiting for me."

"I remember what you told me the first time we met, and I need to make sure you're okay, so I really need you to come have a bite with us. Call Mary and let her know. You can use the phone in my office."

I called Mary and told her I was invited out to eat. She told me not to worry but to call her when I left because she would be up.

"You always go to bed early."

"I'll be awake. Call me."

When I was ready to leave the restaurant, I was still feeling shaky. Sure I now knew that I was gay and that this preacher believed I wasn't going to Hell, but I still doubted that I wasn't in trouble with God and still believed that I might be going to Hell.

Pastor Tina made sure that I called Mary, and Mary made sure to say, "So I'll see you in twenty minutes. Are you okay?"

"I'll be home soon."

Pastor Tina hugged me and said, "Don't disappoint Mary; she is waiting for you." It seemed as if they both understood that I was on shaky ground.

Mary was awake and waiting when I got home. I told her that I was gay, and she immediately hugged me and asked again, "Are you okay?"

"I don't know."

"I am here for you, always."

"I know."

After all the years of loving, hugging, kissing, caressing, and feeling guilty after we had been intimate, that night when we made love, I was fully present and didn't feel the same shame I had always felt.

Mary held my hand as she had always done, and as we were falling asleep she said, "I have always loved you and will always be in love with you."

"I have always loved you and have always been in love with you too," I replied.

"FINALLY!" she said, and we drifted off to sleep.

A Moment of Grace

I have always felt guilty that my struggle to come out affected Mary on many levels. She lived with depression and guilt as we prayed for her to be healed, but that healing never happened because it wasn't needed. God didn't need to heal her. Her sexuality is not a sin in God's eyes. I know I couldn't have known until I could finally know. I am trying to give myself grace and remember that God uses our struggles in mighty ways.

24
I Died at Age Thirty

I tell people that I died the night I came out. The fake me died, and I experienced a rebirth into the authentic me. Finally, I had outwardly claimed my sexuality: I was gay. Living with the realization that I was a lesbian, however, and finding the courage to reclaim my faith, would be a whole other journey.

After thirty long years of unknowing, I was ready to be out! At the same time, I still wasn't sure whether I was in trouble with God. Sure, this one preacher believed I wasn't going to Hell, but everyone has their own opinions and beliefs, and I still believed that I might be going to Hell.

I started telling my siblings, and each one said the same thing: "Yeah, I know. I was just waiting for you to tell me." *Really?* I also called friends and people I worked with whom I trusted. But I didn't feel safe telling my parents face-to-face, so I opted to write them a letter. It took me days to write it. The pen shook in my hand as I tried to tell them that I was gay. The first draft was six pages long before I could even say the word "gay." Doubt crept back in. *If I can't say the word, am I really gay?* My stomach was in knots as I crumbled up page after page of rewrites until I had a two-page coming out letter that expressed my love for them and told them I was gay. I emphasized that Mary had nothing to do with the feelings I already had for her, explaining that I believed I had always been gay and just couldn't admit it to myself.

After I mailed the letter, I felt as if I was holding my breath waiting for a response. Two weeks later, I mentioned to my sister Polly that I had mailed the letter and was waiting to hear back.

"That's rude. They should've called you by now."

"I don't want them to call me if they aren't ready."

Well, that wasn't good enough for Polly, who called my parents and told Momma that she should call me.

Unfortunately for Mary, I was out shopping when Momma finally called. Mary was on the phone with her for an hour while Momma blamed her and accused her of turning me gay. When I got home, Mary told me that Momma was waiting to hear from me. As I dialed the number, my heart skipped a beat, my stomach flipped, and a feeling of dark dread came over me.

"Hello," Momma answered.

"Hey Momma, it's Midge."

"We got your letter. I can't believe you did this to us. How selfish! You know, your father threw it across the room and hasn't spoken about it since. I know you aren't gay. It's just because you like Mary so much. You need to move away from her. You aren't gay."

"I am gay, Momma. This has nothing to do with Mary. I had a crush in middle school, and I had a crush in college."

"You were engaged to Blake and you loved Henry when y'all dated."

"Yes, that's true, but the engagement was a panic move. Henry and I do love each other, but not in that way."

"I don't believe it, and you are going to Hell for this. You can't go to Heaven if you're gay. That's an abomination."

"Then I guess I'm going to Hell, because this is who I am, and I am learning that the Bible may not say that for sure."

"Then you better read it again because it is right there in black and white."

"Well, I love you Momma, but I don't know what else to say."

"You have broken our hearts," she said before hanging up.

A few weeks later, Polly gave birth to her first son, so Mary and I showed up to support her. Our first nephew got stuck in the birth canal, and Polly lost so much blood that she required emergency surgery. I called home.

Daddy answered the phone and refused to talk to me when he heard my voice on the line. I called back three times, and he hung up on me every time. On the fourth call, I blurted out, "Polly is dying!" before he had a chance to hang up on me. He handed the phone to Momma.

The next day, my parents showed up at the hospital to see Polly. I knew they were coming and was scared to death to see them. I was sitting in Polly's room when they walked in. Both of them stared at me and then looked past me to talk to Polly. My breathing was shallow, and I stayed quiet.

After talking with Polly, my dad turned back to me and said, "Have you eaten?"

"No."

"Come with us."

"Where are we going?" I really didn't trust where they would take me.

"Where do you think? The cafeteria."

I followed them out of the room and hoped that we really were going to the cafeteria. I had heard stories from friends whose families kidnapped them and put them into psychiatric placements.

When we got to the cafeteria, my parents talked about Polly and never brought up my letter. I was too scared to bring it up. The entire time, I was waiting for something bad to happen. My stomach was cramping, so I only ordered a drink, which Daddy challenged.

"Why aren't you ordering food?"

"You know I hate hospitals. I just thought I'd come down to visit with you, but I'm not really hungry."

He stared at me and then ordered what he and Momma wanted. Even swallowing liquid was hard during that unbearably awkward visit.

Thankfully, that visit ended without anything overtly bad happening, but I knew at that moment that my relationship with my parents would be forever changed.

In the years to come, every visit with my parents was tense and uncomfortable. Daddy was very reactive any time I inadvertently touched Mary's arm, and I was disinvited to family reunions if I wouldn't go along with pretending that I wasn't in a relationship with a woman. It was unbearable at times to be with them, yet I still craved their acceptance and love, and they refused to disown me. It was emotionally exhausting. Looking back, I know that I shut down all my feelings to get through it, and that took a toll on both my body and my soul.

Nevertheless, with or without my family, I was ready to stop wasting time and move on with my life and my relationship with Mary. I couldn't wait to have a Holy Union to signify our love. I didn't want us to be in a relationship without the only union we were allowed to have (still a little religious guilt going on, I think). As it turned out, Mary and I proposed to each other on the same day! The same day I had planned on asking her to marry me was the same day she decided to slip a ring on my finger while we were snuggling on the couch. I couldn't believe it!

We chose to have our ceremony in the backyard of some dear friends in Greensboro, North Carolina. They were so happy for us that they planted 40 rainbow-colored mums alongside a path to the arbor. Rose, who had a minister's license, married us. It was such a beautiful and spiritual day filled with many loving friends. Dani lay beside the arbor, and I traced her paw on the line as our witness.

Though Momma came, Daddy refused to attend because he would not condone our love or support our wedding. I felt hurt and rejected by him, and I was conflicted about Momma's presence at the Holy Union. I was happy she was there to support us, but I knew she thought we were going to Hell, and I didn't want any judgment on our special day.

Mary's dad and my brother walked us down the aisle, respectively. Having my brother there to support us meant the world to me, and I was so happy that he genuinely wanted to be there for us.

My sister refused to let our nephews come to the wedding and carry our bracelets because she didn't want them to witness our union. I disinvited her because of this, but she showed up anyway. Her wanting to support me didn't ease the feeling of her disrespecting my wishes, nor did it address the betrayal of her keeping these boys that Mary and I had loved, spent time with, and baby sat—not to mention had been listed as guardians to—were jerked away from our sacred moment.

A Moment of Grace

I appreciate that my brother, mom, and sister wanted to support Mary and I by attending our Holy Union. I realize that my parents and my sister did not have the knowledge or skills to understand that my being gay was not a choice, and their fear for my salvation interfered with them being able to be fully supportive.

25

Reclaiming My Faith

It took the next 33 years for me to come to a place where I can say with 99 percent assurance that I am gay and that the God of my understanding loves me. The 1 percent that is still very loud at times is the fearful part, which is rooted in the fact that I don't know anything for certain. After all, I still don't know who made God!

Mary was raised in the Methodist church. She has always believed there is a God and that she has a relationship with Him. She did attend Metropolitan Community Church with me sometimes, and she enjoyed the sermons, but her default faith doesn't depend on church. I was raised in church, and that doctrine is hard to release. We visited a Methodist church together when I first moved to Asheboro, but we were stared at and ignored, and we quickly went home. That was the last time we went to church together.

At this point, I began to switch my energy from religion to spirituality. Reading about Buddhism, chakras, energy healing, and alternative ways to live in the world without religion, I began to feel free and unbound by the judgment that I had always felt in church. I focused on feeling worthy and tried to find ways to embrace my own divinity. Meditation and reading books by Dr. Wayne Dyer showed me how to set my intentions and manifest what I desired. I began yoga and meditation with davidji, a certified Vedic Master and creator of guided meditations around the world, which soothed my anxiety and gave me a connection to the Divine—one that didn't need to be called "God."

I felt I was in my flow, and although I was happy, I sensed something was missing. I really missed church and a body of people to worship with. For years I stayed away from church because I didn't want to hear a sermon telling me I would go to Hell. I tried several times to find an affirming church that wasn't too far from where we lived, and I talked to several pastors in town. Each one was kind and welcoming, but each also believed that "homosexuality is a sin."

After many failed attempts over the years, I finally had a conversation with an open and affirming minister in town. Though he encouraged me not to be out in front of the congregation because they were elderly and not affirming, he also said he could promise I would never hear a damnation sermon from him. I started going there and was embraced by the congregation—as long as I kept up my facade of not being gay. I started singing in the choir and eventually became their choir director.

During this time, I was getting weird vibes from the minster. I noticed that he always had to hug everyone, even those who didn't want it. Many things happened that felt wrong, but I ignored them because I was finally back in church.

The day it fell apart was when I stayed late with the minister and his young grandson to help him pack up his truck with donations. While I helped carry things out and put them beside his truck, he was on the phone with his wife. As I turned to wave goodbye, he motioned for me to come back. I came back across the parking lot and, as I got closer, he pulled me to him and kissed me. I pulled away, got into my truck, and sped away as I heard him yell, "Stop! Wait!"

When I got home and told Mary what happened, she was livid.

I was working as a therapist at the time, in a private practice owned by a sex offender specialist. I made a list of all the incidents that had happened that had made me feel uncomfortable. Keeping it anonymous, I handed it to her and said, "Do you think this person is in trouble?"

She immediately said, "These are grooming behaviors. Whoever is experiencing this is going to be in big trouble soon. They need to get away from this person."

She must have seen the change in my demeanor because she then asked, "Is this you? Who is this person?"

I explained what was happening, and she suggested I get out immediately. There was nothing concrete to report, but his behavior was highly inappropriate and abusive.

Though I wrote a letter to a deacon of the church, describing my concerns and what had occurred, I never heard back. After I left the church, the minister called me every day for a week to try to persuade me into changing my story. I finally told him, "If you call me one more time, I will call the police and tell them you are harassing me." He stopped calling.

That was the last church I attended until I found the Episcopal Church of the Good Shepherd in 2019. The business Mary and I worked out of closed, and while I still felt called to serve in a therapeutic context, I didn't want to continue doing the same work I had done for over 30 years. And so, I opened my own online coaching business and started working from home.

A few months after that, a friend of mine asked if I would help her start an LGBTQIA+ spirituality/support group for people in our community. We were looking for a meeting space, and some other friends suggested the Episcopal Church. They said that the priest would probably let us use the space for free. My first reaction was, "Are you crazy?

How am I going to tell a group of people who have been abused and wounded by the church that we're going to meet at a church?"

"Just meet him; you'll see," they said.

As fate would have it, I was introduced to the priest, Father Joe Mitchell, at a local fundraising event. We scheduled a time during his office hours to talk at the local coffee shop. I thought that was a cool way to meet, but I was terrified to speak with a priest. Old messages from Paw Paw told me that Catholics were going to Hell, and they loomed in my mind. I didn't know that Episcopalians also had priests. For an hour and a half, I tried to trip him up with all my fundamentalist questions to see if he was—as I suspected—another minister in a long line of ministers who welcome homosexual "deviants" into the church just to pray for their sins. I was surprised to leave that meeting feeling heard, seen, and affirmed.

He outright told me, "Midge, I don't believe you are going to Hell for being gay, and furthermore, I don't believe the Bible says that either."

My face flushed with excitement at hearing that, yet I still felt afraid to believe it.

Father Joe later invited me to an outdoor service called "Mass on the Grass" so that I could get to know people and see what a service was like without actually coming inside the church. It was another moment in my life when I wanted to move forward while simultaneously wanting to run away as fast as I could. I knew I couldn't handle one more disappointment, one more wound from the church, one more broken trust, one more heartbreak. I felt exhausted and broken in a battle between my overactive brain and my soul.

In August of 2019, after months of conversations with Father Joe, I was finally brave enough to attend a Mass on the Grass service. I really loved the experience and started attending regularly. We had set up our LGBTQIA+ group, and Father Joe allowed us to use the church's kitchen and parlor for our meetings. Many of my friends who wanted to attend were already members of the church, so it worked out great.

Still, I feared being in the main sanctuary. When it got too cold for outdoor services, they were held in the small chapel. Convincing myself that it was like camp, not church, I sat in the back pew. I was comforted by Father Joe's dog and the church chaplain, Casey, who realized I needed emotional support. I took the Episcopal 101 classes to learn more about the denomination and had several more meetings with Father Joe.

The day I decided to attend church in the actual sanctuary, my heart was pounding, my hands were shaking, and I felt sick to my stomach (hence the original subtitle for this memoir!) All of my past wounds were being exposed again, and it wasn't easy. I was scared to death to trust, and I couldn't bear it if it didn't work out. Nevertheless, I started to lean in and was affirmed and accepted by all I met at the parish.

Then, on November 9th, 2019, a neighbor's dog attacked our beloved Corgi, Roddie, along with Mary and our other dogs. When the neighbor got his dog's mouth off Roddie's leg, Roddie ran past our house and into the woods. I was at our mountain cabin getting ready to run a women's retreat when I got the news. My race home was the longest hour and 45 minutes I have ever experienced. When I got there, Mary and I walked through creeks, woods, and freezing rain, constantly calling his name. We put up hundreds of signs and had many friends, neighbors, and community members rally around us, giving us donations, bringing us food, supporting us, and walking with us. One blessed parishioner at Good Shepherd, who had attended the healing service with me, abandoned her own family every day to walk with me, listening to me rail against God and question everything. Her faith and her determination to be my church in those muddy creeks was a powerful testimony.

I continued to rage against God in meetings with Father Joe, who always supported without judgment. One day I defiantly asked if there was a saint Episcopalians prayed to for lost dogs, and he quickly said, "St. Anthony, the saint of lost things." When I told him I didn't know what to pray for, he gently said, "Sometimes our tears are the only prayers we need. God knows our hearts."

In early December, I was in my truck with my friend from the healing service when my phone alerted me to a missed message. I was tired and didn't want to follow up on what I assumed was another spam call, but my friend insisted I call the number back because, "You never know!"

It turned out that someone had found Roddie and left their phone number and address for us to come get him. I called Mary and exclaimed, "We got a call from someone who said they found Roddie in their woods!" Mary stayed on the phone with me as I raced to the location.

When I got there and jumped out of my truck, I saw a small face looking at me from a hole in a board across the porch. "Roddie, is that you?" I asked. Barely able to control my excitement, I raced down the hill and picked up this filthy, emaciated dog that barely looked like Roddie but still had on his collar, tags, and leash. After three-and-a-half weeks, our boy was finally home. He was in bad shape, but he was alive, and he got healthier every day. My daily spiritual search buddy and I went back to church, and I was confirmed an Episcopalian on February 9th, 2020.

COVID-19 brought the world to a standstill soon after I was confirmed; we all had to pause and live out our faith without going to church. Father Joe made sure we could still meet on Facebook Live, but shortly after that he began dealing with multiple health issues, and I began to panic. All the messages of my unworthiness loomed overhead, as I felt I had brought all of this on the church and beloved Father Joe because I, the gay girl, dared to return to church! I realize now that that sounds dramatic, but for most of my life I was told that I was an abomination, so I felt responsible for all the bad things that were happening.

After I spoke with Father Joe one day and he said, "Midge, you are not that powerful," I had to laugh and put it all into perspective.

I started the practice of spiritual direction during the pandemic, which was a Godsend. Spiritual direction has given me a safe space to grieve the loss of my faith, process my anger at God, and clarify that I am not an abomination. I have learned to use tools such as the Centering Prayer to connect with God on a deeper level, and I have embraced a new way of looking at sin as just missing the mark rather than something that will send me to Hell. I have learned that many decisions I have made have been callings that I was brave enough to answer instead of knee jerk reactions that seemed reckless, and I've learned that my faith is not contingent on the building I worship in or whether Father Joe is there. My faith is within me, and it is enhanced when I get to worship and take Holy Eucharist alongside a body of people who affirm that I am God's beloved.

It has taken me 63 years to get to the place I am right now. When I look back on my life, I feel deep sadness, some regret, and awe that I have survived. I have been my own worst enemy at times yet, through it all, God has been constant and the Holy Spirit has moved in and through me, even when I didn't recognize it.

I have learned that I am God's beloved, even when I didn't know it, even when I didn't think I wanted to be, and even in my resistance, anger, doubts, and confusion. My journey doesn't have a destination on this earth. I will always be learning, stretching, and growing into a deeper relationship with the God of my understanding. I *am* gay with God, which means that I embrace my authentic lesbian self with pride *and* am a Christian who strives every day to walk the walk of Jesus. When I miss that mark, I deal with the old messages of condemnation and remember that I am not condemned for being human.

I am shifting from judging myself harshly and condemning myself when I mess up to giving myself the compassion and grace that I extend to others. Do I still doubt and question? Do I still have moments of fear and suicidal ideations? Yes, but not as often as I did in the past. I am still wounded, yet I know my wounds don't define me. With God's help, my trials have forged me into a strong, authentic, compassionate person who is now able to shed a light onto someone else's dark path and offer hope.

> ### A Moment of Grace
>
> For all those who have wounded me (and for the man whose dog attacked my family), may you experience God's agape love. All of us do the best we can with what we know at the time. No one can give away what they don't have, so I choose to give myself grace and compassion.

Epilogue

Once it became legal in North Carolina, my beloved and I were married on December 6th, 2014. Our lives have been full of love, laughter, and loss.

We have built a sacred cabin in the mountains of North Carolina where we can unplug and be away from all the chatter of life. That space has welcomed many friends and offered solace to those in need. Our lives have also been enriched by the heartbeats of so many fur babies since Dani and Sheba. That could be an entire memoir, which a friend has already, jokingly, named *GAY with DOGS!*

As a couple, Mary and I have had our dark nights of the soul. We have faced challenges that could have ended our journey together, but we have always come back to the deep love that connected our souls back in that little office at ASU. We still fall asleep at night holding hands and know that our love will never die.

When I received the first round of edits for this memoir, I freaked out. "My book sucks!" I ranted to Mary. "I don't know what I'm doing!"

2023

Mary held me close as I cried. "It doesn't suck," she assured.

"How do you know? You haven't read it."

"I know because you're a good writer, and you don't give up on things that are important to you. You will do this. I believe in you." That is the deep love between us that has been the one constant in my life.

My devoted spiritual director has sustained me through the toughest times in my faith journey, helping unpack my religious wounds and offering me hope that I am not bound by misinformation. She was so valuable during the height of the pandemic when I couldn't attend church and has been my guide as I clarify my relationship with God and the Bible.

I am learning to give myself grace, which I quickly extend to others, and to see God and the Bible more realistically. I cannot say enough

EPILOGUE

about Father Joe, who has walked with me through my ugliness and has always extended me God's love.

Mary still finds her relationship with God outside of church. I find deep solace with God in silence and while in connection with the beloved people I worship alongside. The Episcopal Church of the Good Shepherd has given me the opportunity to spread my spiritual wings. I have helped out with the tech team, live-streaming our services and assisting our formation class to meet on Zoom. I am a Lector, a Eucharistic Minister, a member of the Pastoral Care Team, and currently a member of the vestry. I am open to wherever the Holy Spirit leads.

I am also serving our LGBTQIA+ community through my coaching practice, through my *GAY with GOD!* podcast, and through several Facebook groups. This memoir is an offering to all of you who are still searching.

My coming out was far from easy, and it took me 30 years to do it. My faith journey has found some solid ground, and although I still get triggered and deal with challenges, I am better equipped not to run from God. Instead of my initial reaction of "OMG," I now have daily conversations with God and lean into silence to listen.

My memoir has been written, but my life story is not over. I have always said, "As long as I am still above ground and still breathing, I am not done!"

Afterword

Saint Irenaeus of Lyons once wrote, "The glory of God is a human being fully alive."[4]. I have always interpreted this to mean that when we are our most authentic selves, God's glory is revealed in us and through us. This is why Jesus of Nazareth is often seen as the most authentic, most human being that has ever lived, because it is in him and through him that God's glory is revealed.

As I have walked with Midge on her spiritual journey, I am often reminded of the ways she lives into this saying. From the first time we chatted in that coffee shop on a Monday morning—Lord only knows exactly how long that conversation lasted!—she has been nothing less than her authentic self, one of the most fully alive human beings I have been blessed to know. Such authenticity takes a tremendous amount of courage and a willingness to be vulnerable, brave, and bold. Midge displays such courage whenever she speaks truth to power, shares her story with others, and stands tall when she proclaims that you can, in fact, be gay with God. It is beautiful and inspiring to witness, and I am blessed to have been a part of her story.

I have, sadly, heard it said to those struggling with their sexual orientation or gender identity that God does not make mistakes, and therefore the way that they are—or rather, the way they perceive themselves to be—is not part of God's plan. To that I say, indeed, God does not make mistakes; in fact, the way you are is exactly how God made you and exactly how God's glory will be revealed in you! Whether gay, bisexual, transgender, nonbinary, pansexual, or whatever identity or orientation you may claim, that is exactly who God made you to be, and God loves you just the way you are! By virtue of simply being who you are, by being your most authentic self, by being "fully alive," you give to those around you a small glimpse at the wonder and beauty of our loving, liberating, and life-giving God. This is the very Good News that Jesus came to offer us: that God so loved the whole human race that He just had to come and be a part of it.

If Midge's story has managed to remind even one person of the love God has for them—especially someone whose own friends, family, and pastors may have said otherwise—then this memoir has fulfilled its purpose, to which I say to Midge, "Well done, thou good and faithful servant!"

But Midge's story isn't done. I suspect there is a reason that she concludes this memoir with her coming to the Episcopal Church, being elected to the Vestry (our congregational council), and serving regularly as both a proclaimer of the Word (a lector) and bearer of the Sacrament (a Eucharistic Minister). Surely it is to remind all of us that saying yes to God is only the beginning. Contrary to what some may preach, our purpose in life is not to go out and "get saved" and therefore have our "Get out of Hell free" card stamped for when we die. Our purpose is to walk daily with Jesus, to walk in the way of love, to remember that we are in this thing together, and that it is only by loving, praying, and working together that we are collectively saved. And, rather than wish

AFTERWORD

for Heaven when we die, we can help show others, as Jesus himself reminds us, the "the kingdom of Heaven has come near." No one does this alone.

As I watch Midge continue to live into the faithful person that she is, discerning each day where God is leading her and what ways she can show God's love to others, I see someone who is not trying to be perfect but faithful. And being faithful means simply saying yes to God each day because God has already said yes to you!

Remember, dear reader, that as The Most Reverend Michael Curry (Presiding Bishop of the Episcopal Church) often says, "If it ain't about love, it ain't about God!" Blessedly, Midge Noble found her way to that Gospel truth. It does not mean that her life beforehand was wasted; far from it. Like the story of Joseph (he of the FABULOUS technicolor dreamcoat!), Midge may have faced serious hardships along the way, but it has all led her to this moment. For that she can say, to borrow the words of my favorite songwriter, "Thank you for what I became!"

May you, too, have the courage to become who you are—who God has always known you to be. May you find in Midge's story of faith, hope, and love those same qualities in your life so that no matter who you are, you may never forget that you are beautifully made in the image of One who loves you more than you can possibly imagine! Thank you, Midge, for reminding us all of this everlasting truth.

The Reverend Joe Tyler Mitchell, a.k.a. "Father Joe"

Closing Letter

Dear Reader,

Thank you for taking the time to read my memoir. You have honored me by reading it. I hope my story gives you the courage to keep moving forward if you are struggling to come out, have had thoughts of suicide during this process, and feel you cannot be a gay Christian. I hope you understand that God loves you because you are gay, and I hope you feel empowered to lean into your own faith journey. There are people who can help you. You are not alone.

You *can* claim to be the person you have been created to be. It may be hard, and you may sometimes feel lost in the process, but you *can* do it.

To my family, friends, and all the lives that I have crossed paths with on my journey, I want you to know that I love you. I wrote my story with authenticity and honored my memories. You may not agree with how I remember them, but they are my memories and I have told them from my own experience.

Thank you for being a part of my journey.

Namaste,

Midge

Acknowledgments

It is with deep love that I thank my beloved wife for all your support and belief in me. I cherish our love. You gifted me with an unwavering love when I didn't love myself, and even when I couldn't openly love you on the level you deserved. The sacrifices you have made in loving me have not gone unnoticed. You are my soulmate and my forever love.

Please indulge me as I give a shout out to the fur babies and angels that have to date enriched our lives: Sheba, Dani, Rainie, Secha, Karysa, Layla, Echo, Roddie, and Jasper. Currently our pack is thriving with Mona Belle, Ella B., Kona, Kenzie, and Dakota. Such a selfless and holy love they give.

A big hug to my cousin from Virginia who rescued Ella and did not take no for an answer. Our daily conversations always bring me a smile and lift me up, and I can feel the luv!

Thank you to my cousin, who offered her photography expertise so that I could upgrade my website and have a decent picture of myself for the book cover.

A special shout out to those of you who have had an integral part in supporting this memoir: Charles and Chris, who planted the seeds and believed in this project before I ever considered writing a memoir; the PYP staff, my PYP writing buddy, and members of the PYP Author Lab and writing academy; and my Facebook dream team. Your support has made this memoir accessible and book-ready!

To Sharon L., who has lovingly and painstakingly read, reread, edited, and offered suggestions for this book and has been brave enough to rework my ramblings. I could not have finished this memoir without you.

To Kristen M., who in the 11th hour gave of your time and talents to propel my memoir forward in profound ways.

To my editor who understood my voice better than I did at times and believed my story was worthy to be heard.

To my proofreader that cut through my emotional words and brought clarity and consistency to my story, I love how you do what you do.

To our dear besties who have supported us throughout our journey, thank you for your love and support.

To Martha L., who proofread the final copy to make sure we caught all the mistakes, "Thank you!...I hope we did!"

To Julia, thank you for capturing my vision and providing my awesome book cover.

To Kree, thank you for quickly updating my website and providing a pre-order component.

ACKNOWLEDGMENTS

To my family who have suffered, laughed, and cried with me throughout our lives. I love you all even though we still have our moments.

To my dear friends who know we are family, and to my Good Shepherd family, thank you from the bottom of my heart for your unwavering love and support. You have sustained me when I really wanted to quit and didn't think I could move forward.

To Father Joe, Kristen, and angel Casey. I would not be where I am spiritually without your presence in my life. You all walk the walk and talk the talk of Jesus. You have shown me God's love in action, provided a safe space for all my questions, and encouraged me to lean into a more meaningful relationship with the God of my understanding. Namaste.

About the Author

Midge Noble is an online resiliency coach, speaker, podcaster, and author of two children's books titled *SHEBA: Home Is Where Your Heart Is* and *Ice Cube Award: Learning to Be Cool Under Pressure*. Her most recent book is a memoir titled *Gay with God: Reclaiming My Faith, Honoring My Story*.

Midge specializes in helping her LGBTQIA+ community in their coming out and faith journeys. Her main focus is to stop gay suicides by educating people wounded by the church that they can be in a relationship with the God of their understanding and that God does and has always loved us, just as we are created to be. To that end, Midge is very involved in her parish, The Episcopal Church of the Good Shepherd.

Midge and her wife, along with their fur babies, enjoy spending time at their mountain cabin, hiking, and being with their friends.

Connect with Midge

To my readers, I love hearing from you. Please feel free to use my email to let me know how my story resonated with you: empoweredmidge@gmail.com

You can also connect with me through social media:

My website: https://gaywithgod.com
Facebook: https://www.facebook.com/midge.noble4
Instagram: @Midge.Noble

Listen to The Podcast

The church tells us we can't be Christian and gay.

The church is wrong.

The truth is, we *can* be gay and have a relationship with the God of our understanding.

The faith journey stories shared in this podcast are powerful, inspiring, and poignant. *GAY with GOD!* is a safe place to hear the truth about who you are created to be and to realize that being gay with God is your birthright.

I welcome you. You belong here. Visit https://empoweredmidge.podbean.com/ and become part of the *GAY with GOD!* community!

Hire Midge

If you need support on your coming out or faith journey, please reach out for a complimentary session with me at <u>Complimentary Session</u>.

You can find out more about working with me on my website at gaywithgod.com

Gay With God
Book Club Questions

1. Midge struggled with feelings of unworthiness for most of her life. Have you experienced feelings of unworthiness, either generally, spiritually, or professionally?
2. Midge was raised to believe that the Bible is the inspired word of God and that it can't be questioned. What beliefs about the Bible were you taught? Do these still ring true for you today?
3. As she was growing up, Midge experienced deep feelings for girls but couldn't identify them as romantic crushes. How early did you know you were not straight? Feel free to share your coming out experience with the group.
4. If you are a parent, teacher, or ministry leader with an LGBTQIA+ child, when did you recognize or have a feeling that they may not be straight?

5. Midge often struggled with doubts and fears regarding God and her salvation. What faith struggles are you experiencing or have you experienced in your relationship with the God of your understanding?
6. Feeling triggered by the word "God," Midge felt safer using "Creator of All That Is." How do you relate to the God of your understanding?
7. Midge grew out of her fear and shame surrounding religion and now has a deeper relationship with the God of her understanding. How has your relationship with the God of your understanding changed over time?
8. It was a lifelong journey for Midge to hear God's call and align with it. When you hear people talking about hearing God's call, how does that feel? How do you believe God calls or speaks to you today? (I still want the burning bush!)

Bibliography

Bray, Anna Eliza. *Traditions, Legends, Superstitions, and Sketches of Devonshire: On the Borders of the Tamar and the Tavy, Illustrative of Its Manners, Customs, History, Antiquities, Scenery, and Natural History*, Volume II. London: John Murray, 1838.

Lamott, Anne. *Bird by Bird: Some Instructions on Writing and Life*. New York: Anchor Books, 1994.

OWN. "The Powerful Lesson Maya Angelou Taught Oprah." Oprah's Life Class. Originally aired October 19, 2011. https://www.oprah.com/oprahs-lifeclass/the-powerful-lesson-maya-angelou-taught-oprah-video.

Lyons, Iraneous. *Against Heresies*. Book 4, Chapter 20, Section 7. Circa 185 A.D. Republished by Beloved Publishing, LLC 2014.

The B Corp Movement

Dear reader,

Thank you for reading this book and joining the Publish Your Purpose community! You are joining a special group of people who aim to make the world a better place.

What's Publish Your Purpose About?
Our mission is to elevate the voices often excluded from traditional publishing. We intentionally seek out authors and storytellers with diverse backgrounds, life experiences, and unique perspectives to publish books that will make an impact in the world.

Beyond our books, we are focused on tangible, action-based change. As a woman- and LGBTQ+-owned company, we are committed to reducing inequality, lowering levels of poverty, creating a healthier environment, building stronger communities, and creating high-quality jobs with dignity and purpose.

As a Certified B Corporation, we use business as a force for good. We join a community of mission-driven companies building a more equitable, inclusive, and sustainable global economy. B Corporations must meet high standards of transparency, social and environmental performance, and accountability as determined by the nonprofit B Lab. The certification process is rigorous and ongoing (with a recertification requirement every three years).

How Do We Do This?
We intentionally partner with socially and economically disadvantaged businesses that meet our sustainability goals. We embrace and encourage our authors and employee's differences in race, age, color, disability, ethnicity, family or marital status, gender identity or expression, language, national origin, physical and mental ability, political affiliation, religion, sexual orientation, socio-economic status, veteran status, and other characteristics that make them unique.

Community is at the heart of everything we do—from our writing and publishing programs to contributing to social enterprise nonprofits like reSET (https://www.resetco.org/) and our work in founding B Local Connecticut.

We are endlessly grateful to our authors, readers, and local community for being the driving force behind the equitable and sustainable world we are building together.

To connect with us online, or publish with us,
visit us at www.publishyourpurpose.com.

Elevating Your Voice,

Jenn T Grace

Jenn T. Grace
Founder, Publish Your Purpose

Printed in the USA
CPSIA information can be obtained
at www.ICGtesting.com
LVHW022139041023
760082LV00010B/326/J